On
Anxiety

'. . . a deft application of psychoanalytic insights to very everyday and quite familiar human situations . . . a revealing and insightful way of looking at the contemporary world where they are imaginatively viewed through the lens of anxiety.'

Juliet Flower MacCannell, University of California

Praise for the series

RENATA SALECL

On
Anxiety

Routledge
Taylor & Francis Group

LONDON AND NEW YORK

First published 2004
by Routledge
2 Park Square, Milton Park, Abingdon, Oxon, OX14 4RN

Simultaneously published in the USA and Canada
by Routledge
270 Madison Ave, New York, NY 10016

Reprinted 2006

Routledge is an imprint of the Taylor & Francis Group

Typeset in Joanna MT by
RefineCatch Limited, Bungay, Suffolk
Printed and bound in Great Britain by
TJ International Ltd, Padstow, Cornwall

British Library Cataloguing in Publication Data
A catalogue record for this book is available from the British Library

Library of Congress Cataloging in Publication Data
A catalog record for this book has been requested

ISBN 0-415-31275-2 (hbk)
ISBN 0-415-31276-0 (pbk)

For Tim

Contents

One

One often hears that we live in an age of anxiety. With the turn of the new millennium, it looks as if the scientific research, economic development, military interventions and the power of the new media are less and less under public control, and that all kinds of catastrophes can be envisioned in the future.[1] In the last months of the old millennium, people already experienced this anxiety when they were bombarded with the danger of the millennium bug. While politicians gave warning to the people to prepare themselves for the possible collapse of computer systems, it looked very much like no one was in charge any more in today's society. The fear of possible catastrophes, however, quickly turned into a search for the conspirators: when it was clear that there was no millennium bug, a theory emerged that the whole fuss around it was created by the computer companies to enable them to sell more advanced computers.

When we talk about the new age of anxiety we should not forget that in the last century it was always the case that after some major social crisis there came the age of anxiety. This happened especially after the wars. In the last century, we had the first age of anxiety after the First World War when the use of the new weapons of destruction that came with the Second Industrial Revolution resulted in a radical questioning of the values of modern civilization. In The Crisis of the Mind,[2] Paul

Valery described that in the modern epoch the most dissimilar ideas seemed to coexist freely and that there ceased to be any fixed reference for living and learning. So, even when the military crisis was over, economic crisis remained, and most importantly with it the 'crisis of the mind', which all contributed to anxiety. Europeans especially felt anguish in regard to their existence, since some perceived that they were entering times of meaninglessness. Some too saw as the main cause of the overwhelming feeling of anxiety the death of all modern idols: it looked that man was very much alone, since he had lost belief in God. However, equally important was the loss of the belief in science, progress and reason. This also looked like the death of Europe. The times of anxiety there, however, opened up the space for new totalitarian leaders. Italian fascism and Hitler's rise to power in Germany were particular attempts to find a solution for the age of anxiety. Their politics, however, greatly contributed to the emergence of the second age of anxiety in the last century. After the Second World War we thus again had the age of anxiety, which was especially precipitated by the experience of the Holocaust and Hiroshima. Again, weapons of mass destruction, which resulted in most brutal violence, heightened the feeling of anxiety emerging after the war was over. And then, too, economic crisis became coupled with the crisis of man trying to figure out the idea of the future. This talk of anxiety, however, diminished with the 1960s which ushered in the 'age of abundance'.

Needless to say, the latest age of anxiety concerns the fact that in the 1990s we witnessed the most brutal forms of violence, and that in the last few years we have been dealing with new wars and the evils of the twenty-first century – terrorist attack and the threat of the use of deadly viruses.

These dangers seem to be especially horrible because they appear undead – there are no quick medical or military solutions capable of eradicating them, and although they can constantly multiply they remain invisible. When Bin Laden was perceived by the Americans as the utmost figure of evil, one Chinese trader on the streets of New York nicely depicted his uncanny character, and, amidst the tee shirts that imitated search warrants from the old Western movies with logos 'Bin Laden – dead or alive', displayed a bunch of shirts that stated 'Bin Laden – dead and alive'.

Although it appears that the new age of anxiety is linked primarily to the danger of terrorist attacks and new illnesses, we should not forget that anxiety arises from the changed perception the subject has of him- or herself as well as from changes to their position in society at large. In the last few years, the media have been constantly reporting new psychological disorders. Some of the new syndromes were quite peculiar: in the 1990s, a number of newly rich Americans supposedly suffered from so-called 'sudden wealth syndrome', which is also sometimes referred to as 'affluenza'; young children whose parents were too protective were in danger of developing 'adventure deficit disorder'; and women's magazines were writing about 'body dysmorphic disorders' of people who are too concerned about their looks. Moreover, the list of these disorders seems to be growing rapidly. Anything that is perceived as an impediment to the subject, who is supposed to be fully in control of herself, constantly productive and also not disturbing to society at large, is quickly categorized as disorder. While the subject's inner turmoil and dilemmas in regard to social expectations quickly get named as anxieties. Even before September 11, anxiety became used in the most expansive way. The *New York*

Times,[3] for example, reported from the New York Fashion Week that the editors of fashion magazines experienced 'shoe anxiety' at the show. The article did not make it clear whether the editors felt anxious because of what they saw on the catwalk, or because they themselves wore bad shoes, or they simply did not know which shoes to choose out of their huge collections at home.

Rollo May[4] in his study of anxiety in the twentieth century points out that before 1945 there existed 'covert anxiety' and after 1945 'overt anxiety'. But both public attitudes towards anxiety pointed in a similar direction: they stressed the loneliness of the subject, his or her inability to love or be loved, pressure towards conformity, as well as a particular feeling of 'homelessness' of the individual. May points out that signs of 'covert anxiety' frequently hinge on the issue symbolically expressed in Thomas Wolfe's novel, *You Can't Go Home Again*.[5] The meaning of this inability to go home is supposed to be related to the subject's difficulty in accepting psychological autonomy. Linked to this are the subjects' desperate attempts to divert themselves with excessive activity both at the workplace and in their free time. Anxiety that emerged in the late 1920s, was, of course, linked to economic depression; however, economic insecurity was interrelated with the insecurity that people began to have in their private lives, and there seemed to be a confusion in the roles people were supposed to adopt. Lynds's famous study of life in so-called Middletown pointed out that in the late 1920s people were particularly alienated, because on the one hand they were subjected to the compulsive need to work, the pervasive struggle to conform and the frantic endeavor to cram their leisure time with constant activity, while on the other hand they were caught in the chaos of conflicting patterns with regard to cultural requirements. Dealing with change and uncertainty in all sectors of life at once became in Lynds's view so intolerable that people started embracing rigid and conservative economic and social ideologies.

After the Second World War, the anxiety became overt, since people not only became openly afraid of all kinds of possible new catastrophes (for example those related to atomic warfare), but also became even more insecure about their social roles. Robert Jay Lifton saw a particular problem in the very multiplicity of possibilities that arose for the subject at that time, since the subject was horrified by possible new wars, and also came under pressure to continually change her identity, and this too provoked a particular feeling of anxiety. This anxiety related to diffuseness of identity however contributed to a particular quest for certainty, which is expressed in 'fundamentalist religious sects and various totalistic spiritual movements'.[6]

One can easily say that today's new age of anxiety is very similar to those of the previous two ages. In today's culture, it again seems that economic uncertainty is not the primal cause of anxiety, since the latter is much more connected to the problems people experience with regard to their social roles, to the constant desire to change their identities, and the impossibility of finding any guidance for their action. These uncertainties today also result in people turning to religious fundamentalism and to their embracing social restrictions, which introduce new forms of totalitarianism.

Before September 11 Westerners could have easily embraced the perception that they lived in a world of simulacra in which everything was changeable and in which life looked like a computer game. People thus had the hope that with a proper genetic code and the invention of new drugs matters of life and death would be more predictable and controllable in the future. But September 11 changed this optimism: suddenly both the human body and society itself appeared much more vulnerable again. What especially caused an overwhelming anxiety to emerge was the collapse of the fantasy structures that seemed to organize people's perception of the world and the emergence of two uncanny agents – terrorism and the virus.

In the aftermath of the Second World War we had similar attitudes towards danger. If we look back at the times of the greatest tensions between America and the Communist states, we can observe how both parties perceived anxiety as related to the danger coming from outside, and one response to this were various conspiracy theories.[7] In America in the 1950s there was great fear of Communist conspiracy, and this was reflected in a special way in the horror films from that time. Communism was perceived as a parasite that could invade the social body or as deadly bacteria that could enter every pore of society. Horror films pictured the danger coming into society from the outside either in the form of extra-terrestrials or as some strange external phenomenon that captures humans and replaces them with alien doubles, as in the film *Invasion of the Body Snatchers* (Don Siegel, 1956). The social paranoia of that time also centred on the anxiety of being brainwashed through Communist ideological indoctrination, which would involve various forms of psychological control. At the same time, the Communist East feared infiltration by foreign spies and the ideological control coming from the West in forms of bourgeois consumerism and entertainment.

In the late 1970s and early 1980s a radical change happened in the perception of anxiety when the object of horror became more and more located inside society and especially inside the human body. Communists thus started being afraid of the enemy within in the form of dissidents and the youth movement. In the West, the emergence of the virus HIV radically changed the perception of danger and the human body became the ultimate place where the enemy can attack. Thus, in the last decade it looked as if the virus had replaced the bomb as the ultimate danger to humans and the body became perceived at the same time as a possible victim and as a great warrior against this internal danger. At this time, immunology gained enormous power and studies of bacterial and viral threat to the human body often use the military jargon of the 'wars within'. Similarly, one can observe a change in Hollywood horror movies as films like *It Came From Outer Space* (Jack Arnold, 1953) were replaced by *They Came From Within* (David Cronenberg, 1975).

But, after September 11, it seemed as if the virus and the bomb started to act together and follow a very similar pattern. Terrorists appear very similar to viruses and bacteria in that they are at first invisible, then suddenly erupt at one place or another; afterwards they hide again and one never knows how they have multiplied or what mutations they have made after they came under attack. As bacteria became resistant to antibiotics, terrorists, too, seemed to resist the warfare that was supposed to annihilate them.[8]

After September 11 the American government has been keeping the fear of possible new attacks alive by continuously reminding the public of the unpredictable danger that can come from hidden terrorists. Some have even observed a pattern in the way the government uses hints about possible new attacks. In the first months after September 11, new warnings came every three weeks just before the weekend. One is tempted to guess that some psychologist might have advised the government to keep the public alerted to possible danger, so that they would continue with their patriotic support of the government's foreign policies. In the way media speculated about the probable new targets of attacks, one can also discern a particular pattern: there almost seemed to be a competition among the media over who might be first to figure out another possible place of attack. An early example of such speculation was that Disneyland might be such symbolic target; since Disneyland is such an ultimate American fantasy, one is not surprised that Americans envision that an attack on this place would inflict a particularly symbolic wound upon America's self-image. Other envisioned places of attack, however, all centred on the body being the target of violence through contaminated water, air ventilation, food poisoning, etc.

In these speculations about possible sources of danger, we have again an interesting connection between the inside and the outside. Anthrax attacks seem increasingly to be the work of an internal enemy. And there are other points of internal danger erupting together with possible new dangers from the outside, like the so called 'dirty bombs' which can be made out of radioactive materials in wide use in medical and other industrial devices. After September 11 scientists started informing the public (and any possible new terrorists, too) how such bombs could be made, while at the same time, to allay the public's fears, they were claiming that it was unlikely anyone would want to make these bombs, since manufacturing such a device might be lethal for the producer, too. (Here, it seems that they are forgetting that self-sacrifice played an important part in September 11.) However, when the scientists envisioned what kind of damage such a bomb would make, they invoked a particular comparison with the former

Soviet Union: 'Dr. Kelly offered a case study of what might happen if a dirty bomb containing a cobalt food irradiation bar exploded at the southern tip of Manhattan on a day with light wind blowing toward the northeast. He calculated that Manhattan as far north as Central Park would be contaminated at levels similar to those in the permanently closed zone around the Chernobyl power plant. Manhattan would have to be abandoned for decades, Dr. Kelly said.'[9] What kind of comfort is offered us by sciences trying to figure out what the next catastrophe might be? It almost seems as if Dr. Kelly is writing a new screenplay for a blockbuster movie similar to *Independence Day* or *Armageddon*. And the fact that the possible future American catastrophe might look like the one that happened in the former Soviet Union, invokes disturbing memories of past political divides.

The way the terrorist is perceived as a member of a particular cell, in which he knows only a small number of people who are his links but never has an overview of the whole structure of the organization and does not know its actual leaders, very much resembles the logic that operates in the secret services. Former Soviet spies were especially seen as functioning through such cell structures, depending as they do on their members' clear commitment to their cause and their unquestioning obedience to their commanders. But whereas, in the case of the Soviet spies, it became increasingly easy for the West to co-opt them and convince them to work for the Western powers because of their dissatisfaction with the Communist regime or even through pure material greed, in the case of current terrorists this is not so. The latter appear so much more horrible for Western observers because they cannot be 'bought' or convinced to change sides. For a society that is grounded on the disbelief in grand ideologies, the terrorist presents the horrifying reality of a person who still believes in a cause for which he is willing to sacrifice his life. Moreover, since this higher cause does not involve any search for material satisfaction, the terrorist – in contrast to Communist spies – cannot be perceived as someone willing to succumb to old types of seduction, or as someone who might easily change his ideological beliefs.

If in the past the spy has been a person implanted by a hostile power in order to obtain crucial information, today, with the collapse of previous political divides, the implantation takes other forms. The famous TV series *X Files* provides a good fictional example, when the implant became the ultimate danger, which was first imposed from the outside, but then set in motion a dangerous mutation inside. In one of the series, agent Scully realizes that she has a chip implanted in her head, which must be the work of extra-terrestrials. However, when she has the chip removed, a wild metastasis of some kind of a viral cancer happens in her body, which can only be stopped when the chip is back in place. Things get even more complicated when Scully researches a tissue of a corpse of a boy whom she guesses to be an extra-terrestrial. Scully first establishes that the boy's tissue is contaminated by a virus that radically changes DNA, but then realizes that her own DNA has also been changed. When Scully explains to Mulder what she has found, his comment is that the boy must be an extra-terrestrial, but Scully's conclusion is that we ourselves are already extra-terrestrials – the enemy is clearly within. However, there is always much more of a problem when we are dealing with an enemy within and not from outside. After the Oklahoma bombing, it has been hard for Americans to grasp that this crime could have been committed by a young American man, and as a result conspiracy theories emerged that Timothy McVeigh had a chip installed in his buttock through which outside enemies of some kind controlled his actions.

If at the time of the divide between capitalism and Communism the enemy was clearly perceived as someone coming from the outside, in the age of globalized capitalism the enemy takes the form of a wandering terrorist (an image which, in its elusive character, strangely resembles the anti-Semitic one of the dangerous wandering Jew), while at the same time the inner antagonisms that mark Western capitalist societies are perceived in the form of viral dangers.[10]

This talk about the 'new age of anxiety' related to terrorism, has paradoxically incited new fears related to the divisions between the developed world and the undeveloped one, so that for some countries, the greatest fear was that they might fall into the realm of the excluded. After the anthrax panic erupted in the United States, suddenly in Slovenia, a small country in Central Europe, the media reported a number of cases of fake anthrax. For some days, the media were alerting the public about strange letters containing white powder that were being sent to public institutions. The drama was however soon over when it became clear that someone was just making a joke by sending fake anthrax. Nonetheless, in the way Slovenian media reported on these anthrax scares one could discern concern coupled with some kind of narcissistic exultation. When these anthrax cases became the primary news story of the day, it was as if this tiny country was becoming equal in its fears with powerful America. Since Slovenia itself had recently suffered a brief war after seceding from former Yugoslavia, there was also considerable identification with the victims of the World Trade Center (WTC) attack. Slovenians (and Bosnians even more) remembered that they had experienced the kind of suffering when one's whole perception of the world and one's safety collapses.

Even in places where there was no serious expectation of terrorist attack, one can also observe a particular kind of symbolic identification with the victims of September 11, which can also be understood as a desire to belong to the Western world. This desire was especially illustrated in the way some Poles reacted to the news that a number of their compatriots were killed in the WTC. At first the news was that dozens of Poles had been killed there, but when later the number became much smaller, some people in Poland almost reacted with disappointment: it was not that they secretly wished for the death of more Poles, rather that they very much wanted to 'belong' and to count as one of the important European nations. Some Poles perceived having significant casualties in the WTC as a way of gaining the symbolic recognition of being equal to the Western countries that also had lost a number of citizens in the attack. Post-socialist countries have a desperate desire to join the developed world, and at the time of the terrorist attack in America their governments perceived that it was necessary to be as quick as possible in offering support to America, even if the latter might never need their direct help. But at the same time, their publics felt uneasy about American obsession with war, its constant search for new enemies and its ignorance regarding Third World concerns. While the post-socialist countries can often be quite pathetic in their desire to belong to the developed world, the latter also shows extreme ignorance towards them.

This game of seduction that is played between the West and the Third World is most obviously visible in the art world. Third World artists seeking recognition in the Western art world often fail in the attempt. Ilya Kabakov nicely described the tension between Western and non-Western cultures by pointing out that the Western art world is like a fast train that travels through different countries. In these remote places, people stand on the platforms and hope that they will be able to catch the train. However, the train rarely stops and, even if it does, there are no places on the train. Some people nonetheless succeed in climbing aboard the train and then desperately look for empty seats. When a seat by chance turns up and the person sits down, fellow passengers look at the newcomer with disdain and comment: 'Why did you not sit down earlier? And why did you look so desperate – you should have a smile on your face! We are always happy to get new people on board.' This is precisely the game global capital is playing in today's post-socialist world and, with regard to the September 11 attack, many post-socialist countries very much wanted to be perceived as the passengers on the right train. Being on the right train however does not simply consist in expressing compassion for the victims of terror, but also in the desire to be favourably treated by the drivers of the train – global capital.

Since today's weapons of mass destruction heighten our fear of all kinds of possible catastrophe which we had not observed before, and we have constant media warnings about possible new horrors like mass poisoning, infection with contagious diseases, dirty bombs and other nuclear dangers, there is also an increasing demand for remedies for the increased levels of anxiety. When *The New York Times* reported that in the US 'fear is spreading faster than SARS'[11] and that people are as a result massively avoiding Chinese restaurants, it concluded: 'The biggest problem is the unknown. There is nothing out there that says if you take some medicine, you will be fine. . . . Doctors say. "We are busy trying to educate people, but the worried mind doesn't always hear. You have to get rid of the anxiety before the thoughts sink in." '[12] While people are encouraged by the government to buy duct tape to protect themselves from possible air poisoning, and they are wearing masks in order to protect themselves from viruses, the pharmaceutical industry is thriving by selling all kinds of anti-anxiety drugs and other corporations are encouraging Americans to use so-called 'retail therapy' to calm their fears.

This book will analyse the way anxiety operates in today's society by looking behind the media representation of what is supposed to be anxiety-provoking for people. Our first concern will be to examine the difference between anxiety and fear, and here the Freudian and Lacanian take on anxiety will be most important. Since at the beginning of the new millennium, the danger of new wars became the greatest cause of anxiety, we will look in Chapter Two at war anxieties and the traumas that emerge after wars.

Capitalism today increasingly turns the anxieties the media are talking about to its own advantage, while it also produces ever-new insecurities at the work place. Chapter Three will look at the changes that have happened to people's self-perception in times of so called hyper-capitalism and the anxieties the latter relies on.

On top of work, love incites a lot of anxiety feelings for people. That is why Chapter Four will look at what traumatizes us in our intimate relationships, and how men and women differently look at anxiety in their private lives.

Parenting especially appears anxiety-provoking and often parents feel that they are failing in raising their children. Chapter Five will look at such anxiety in the case of a psychotic mother who decided to kill her children in order to save them from her self.

In the last decade, testimony appeared as a way of curing people's traumas and alleviating anxieties but, as Chapter Six will show, the emergence of the testimony industry relates to the general anxieties that we have in regard to the demise of authorities in today's society and the 'fear' that there is no one to hear us anymore in our suffering.

The main thrust of the book will be to look at how anxiety is linked to the way the individual subject deals with his or her split (i.e. inconsistency), and the antagonisms that mark society. There seems to be an attempt in today's society to find a cure for anxiety by constantly exposing the disturbing objects that might incite it (even in contemporary arts, for example, we try to figure out what is anxiety-provoking in death by exposing cadavers). Constant proliferation of anxieties today also open up a desire for quick solutions (in the form of drugs, for example) which will bring us closer to a type of society that is free of anxiety.

While anxiety is today perceived as something one needs to be able to control and hopefully in the long run get rid of – in short, as an ultimate obstacle to the subject's happiness – it is almost forgotten that philosophy and psychoanalysis discussed anxiety as an essentially human condition that may not only have paralysing effects, but also be the very condition through which people relate to the world.

Two

The road along the perimeter of Camp Fenway leads to nowhere. It runs through the middle of nowhere and it seems to come from nowhere. Along this road, far away from the camp, are two aliens to the nothingness: Marine sentries sitting in a foxhole on a cold night, staring at nothing, observing, studying, absorbing the sights, sounds, textures, odours and tastes of nothing. To these Midwestern men of the 24th Marine Expeditionary Unit, the desert in its entirety is a blue void. . . . There is a third man in the foxhole, an unseen man, the enemy. He does not summon fear, but anxiety. Where is he? Show your face. Come out and fight. The more he does not appear, the more the marines think of him. The purpose of the sentry is to protect the camp. So, it is almost perverse to wish for an attack. But the wish is there nevertheless. A marine wants to earn his keep. Without an adversary, he is nothing but a man sitting in a hole on a road between nowhere and nowhere.[1]

This description of the anxiety faced by the American soldiers on the Iraqi front illustrates perfectly what anxiety is like when we face a dangerous situation: it appears that it is the very void, nothingness, that makes us anxious. And in order to deal with this void, the soldier is hoping to actually find an object he might be afraid of, i.e. a clear adversary. However, although such anxiety can be explained by the violence implicit in a war situation, after the war is over and the danger diminishes, soldiers often experience a continuation or even an escalation of anxiety feelings.[2]

A number of veterans from various wars have had to deal with similar dilemmas; in some cases the subject experienced a particular event in the war and this precipitated his breakdown, while in other cases one cannot pinpoint what specifically triggered the subject's traumas (which could have even brought him to the brink of suicide).

Traumatic experiences that people have after being involved in a violent situation have been very important for psychoanalytic studies of anxiety. Furthermore, the emergence of an age of anxiety has also been linked to the traumas that people suffer after society has faced some extreme form of violence. As pointed out in the Introduction, in the last century it was thought that society was entering an age of anxiety after the long wars. Today, the emergence of new wars seems to have, on the one hand, contributed once again to the escalation of anxiety, while on the other hand, we have the perception that future wars might be acted out from such distance that anxiety will become much less of a problem for the soldiers of those wars.

To understand the logic of anxiety, it is important to go back to the pioneering work of Freud, to which Jacques Lacan has added crucial insights by looking at how language and culture shape our feeling of anxiety. This book will use Freud's and Lacan's insights to explain what has happened with anxiety in today's times. When popular media talk about anxiety they often invoke the need to pacify it with the help of drugs or new techniques for relaxation. Psychoanalysis however points out that anxiety is very much linked to the subject's unconscious and thus cannot be undone with simple behavioural changes. This chapter will use examples from war to illuminate the main points of the Freudian and Lacanian take on anxiety and to tackle the question of how today's perceptions of anxiety differ from past ones. Here, it will be especially important to look at the visions of an anxiety-free future society that emerged at the same time as the use of the most destructive weapons in today's armed conflicts.

ANXIETY AND FEAR

The usual perception is that we fear something that we see or hear, i.e. something that can be discerned as an object or a situation. Fear would thus concern what can be articulated, so that we are, for example, able to say: 'I have a fear of darkness' or 'I am afraid of barking dogs'. In contrast, we often perceive anxiety as a state of fear that is objectless, which means that we cannot easily say what it is that makes us anxious. Anxiety would thus be an uncomfortable affect, which is more horrible than fear precisely because it is unclear to us what provokes it. Such a definition of the difference between anxiety and fear might very well be what we think we experience in our daily lives. However, psychoanalysis provides a more complicated view of their differences.

Freud's first theory was that anxiety has to do with the repressed libido.[3] He particularly focused on coitus inter-ruptus, claiming that the repeated prevention to discharge sexual energy leads to anxiety neurosis. For example, if a woman has been sexually aroused and then suddenly the sexual act stops, her sexual excitation will not be discharged and this can lead to anxiety. Similarly, a man who has to stop in the middle of the act without being able to achieve orgasm will be prone to develop anxiety neurosis, especially if this practice repeats itself over a period of time. With this early theory Freud appears to be very oriented towards biology. However, he is already struggling here with the question of how an anxious reaction towards an outside problem is related to an inner anxiety that the subject experiences. Freud answers this dilemma by making the distinction between an affect of anxiety and anxiety neurosis:

> The psyche finds itself in the *affect* of anxiety if it feels unable to deal by appropriate reaction with a task (a danger) *approaching from outside*; it finds itself in the *neurosis* of anxiety if it notices that it is unable to even out the (sexual) excitation originating *endogenously*, – that is to say, it behaves as though it were projecting that excitation outwards.[4]

Freud also points out that affect and neurosis are firmly related, although the first is a quick reaction to an external stimulus, and the latter is the result of dealing long-term with an internal one.

Thirty years later, Freud decided to radically change his theory on anxiety in his famous study *Inhibitions, Symptoms and Anxiety*. Freud first guessed that anxiety signals some danger in reality, but then quickly pointed out that anxiety primarily has to do with expectation of a danger. In this context, anxiety does seem to be without an object and is thus different from fear. Freud also realized that anxiety expectations correspond differently to particular life periods. In infancy anxiety is linked to the subject's inability to process all the excitation, which is coming from the outside and the inside of his or her body. In childhood, the subject is anxious the people on whom he or she depends might withdraw their loving care. In boyhood, the son is afraid of his rival – his father – since he has sexual inclinations towards the mother,[5] but the adult subject seems to be primarily anxious in front of the superego – the punitive voice inside him. Freud also noticed that neurotics continuously behave as if danger situations from earlier periods still exist: but if 'signs of childhood neurosis exist in all adult neurotics',[6] this does not mean that all children who show those signs will necessarily become neurotics in later life.

The most important point about Freud's second theory on anxiety is that anxiety ceased to be regarded as a result of repression but rather as a cause of it. Anxiety becomes taken as an affect, a bodily excitation, which the subject has difficulties dealing with. Often, the subject develops various inhibitions or symptoms as processes of defence against this feeling of anxiety. Inhibitions, for example, try to prevent the subject from finding him or herself in anxiety situations while symptoms might try to replace anxiety affects. However, in some cases of neuroses symptoms can then also incite new anxieties.

Freud's dilemma in studying anxiety has also been: Why are not all reactions to anxiety neurotic? Why are some reactions to danger normal and others neurotic? Or rather, what is the difference between realistic and neurotic anxiety? Freud's answer is that realistic anxiety is about a known danger and neurotic anxiety is about an unknown danger. However, in understanding the unknown danger, we get a clue that anxiety is not simply an objectless fear, but rather a particular reaction to the danger of the loss of an object. So if at first it looks as though in anxiety we have a lack of an object (i.e. we do not know what we are afraid about), Freud suggested that the problem for the subject is not actually the lack of the object, but rather its loss. Here, Freud concluded that anxiety is always related to the threat of castration, and that in the final instance one shall also regard the fear of death as analogous to the fear of castration.

The whole issue of anxiety becomes even more complicated when we take into account that castration is effective already as a threat (i.e. castrating for the subject is the very anticipation of castration), and that the danger that the subject feels over the possibility of the loss of the object masks the fact that the object – in the meaning of the libidinal object of satisfaction – has always already been lost. Freud tackles this complication by asking himself: When can we say that the subject who has been separated from an object is simply experiencing pain in contrast to anxiety? If pain seems to be an actual reaction to the loss of the object, anxiety becomes rather a reaction to the danger, which that loss entails. Thus, when we say that anxiety is an expectation of a possible danger, we can make a final turn here and conclude that in a state of anxiety, the subject is horrified by the very danger that the loss of the object brings to him or her.

Freud's theory that castration is the greatest fear of the subject instigated an extensive debate among his disciples over what kind of a loss the subject is most anxious about. Melanie Klein objected to Freud's interpretation, and insisted that for the subject the most potent source of anxiety is the fear of life itself.[7] Joan Riviere[8] also concluded that all subjects' terrors are fears of some kind of loss and that the subject fears that any loss means total loss. In contrast, Ernest Jones took anxiety as being rooted in the fear of 'aphanisis' – the loss of the capacity for experiencing pleasure in life, especially sexual pleasure.[9]

When Lacan engaged with Freud's theory on anxiety, he made a number of crucial further observations. For Lacan, the subject's relationship with what he calls the 'big Other', the social, symbolic network that the subject is born into, is very important. This Other does not concern only the institutions and rituals that our society is organized around, but the very language that marks the subject as a speaking being. Lacan points out that the subject has a particular anxiety in regard to the Other. However, it is not that the subject has some kind of a castration anxiety in regard to the Other, i.e. that he or she takes the Other as someone who might take something precious from him or her. Lacan points out that the neurotic in particular does not retreat from a castrating Other, but rather from making of his own castration what is lacking to the Other. What does this mean? When psychoanalysis claims that the subject undergoes symbolic castration by becoming a speaking being, this must be understood as the fact that the subject *per se* is empty – nothing by him- or herself – that all the subject's power comes from the symbolic insignia that he or she temporarily takes on. Here we can take the example of a policeman, who might be a nobody, a boring, insignificant man, until he puts on his uniform and becomes a person with power. The subject is therefore castrated, i.e. powerless by himself, and only by occupying a certain place in the symbolic order does he temporarily get some power or status.

The subject is also always bothered by the fact that the Other is inconsistent, that the Other is split, non-whole, which means that, for example, one cannot say what the Other's desire is or how one appears in the desire of the Other. The only thing that can ensure meaning to the Other (and, for example, provide an answer to the question of the desire of the Other) is a signifier. Since such a signifier is lacking, in the missing place comes a sign from the subject's own castration. To the lack in the Other the subject can thus only answer with his or her own lack. And in dealing with his or her lack, as well as with the lack in the Other, the subject encounters anxiety. However, the source of anxiety for the subject is not the lack, but rather the absence of the lack, i.e. the fact that where there is supposed to be lack, some object is present.

ANXIETY AND FANTASY

One way neurotics deal with their anxiety is by creating a fantasy. Fantasy is a way for the subject to cover up the lack by creating a scenario, a story that gives him or her consistency. However, fantasy also helps the subject prevent the emergence of anxiety – i.e. the emergence of the horrible object at the place of the lack.

Let me illustrate this point with the example of the Israeli soldier Ami, who had served in both the Yom Kippur and the Lebanon wars. Ami had been an avid filmgoer in his youth and when he went to the Yom Kippur War, he felt as if he was going to play the part of a soldier in a war movie. This fantasy sustained him throughout the war:

> I said to myself it is not so terrible. It's like a war movie. They're actors, and I'm just some soldier. I don't have an important role. Naturally, there are all the weapons that are in a war movie. All sorts of helicopters, all sorts of tanks, and there's shooting. . . . [But] basically, I felt that I wasn't there. That is, all I had to do was finish the filming and go home.[10]

Later, in the Lebanon War, Ami felt as if he was on a tourist visit, observing pretty villages, mountains, women, etc.

But at some point, the fantasy of being on a tourist excursion or in a movie broke down. This happened when Ami witnessed massive destruction in the Lebanon war and was involved in heavy face-to-face fighting. The last straw was a particularly horrific scene in Beirut, a scene of stables piled with corpses of Arabian racehorses mingled with corpses of people. The scene filled Ami with a sense of apocalyptic destruction, and he collapsed: 'I went into a state of apathy, and I was not functioning.' Ami explains the process as follows: in the Yom Kippur War,

> I put my defence mechanism into operation and it worked fantastically. I was able to push a button and start it up. . . . In Lebanon, the picture was clearer. In the Yom Kippur War, we didn't fight face-to-face or shoot from a short distance. . . . If I saw a corpse, it was a corpse in the field. But here [in Lebanon] everything was right next to me. . . . And of all things, the thing with the horses broke me. . . . A pile of corpses . . . and you see them along with people who were killed. And that's a picture I'd never seen in any movie. . . . I began to sense the reality [that] it's not a movie anymore.[11]

Anxiety emerges when at the place of the lack one encounters a certain object, which perturbs the fantasy frame through which the subject assessed reality. For the soldier Ami, this happened when he saw the pile of dead horses. If Ami was able to observe dead soldiers on the field through the distance of a fantasy frame, which made him believe that he was an outsider just watching a movie, the emergence of the unexpected object – the horses – caused this fantasy to collapse, a collapse which then triggered Ami's breakdown.

ANXIETY AND THE DESIRE OF THE OTHER

With fantasy, the subject creates for him- or herself a protective shield against the lack, while in anxiety the object which emerges in the place of the lack devours the subject – i.e. makes the subject fade. Anxiety is also in a specific way linked to the desire of the Other – what provokes this anxiety is the fact that the desire of the Other does not recognize me, and even if I have the impression that the Other does recognize me, it will not recognize me sufficiently. The Other always puts me into question, interrogates me at the very root of my being.

In the cases of breakdown in war, one observes a special problem that the subject has with the desire of the Other. Psychiatrists have in the past very much taken into account the fact that a soldier's breakdown is often triggered by the change in the basic pattern of the soldier–group relationship: 'This might be an actual change in the structure of the group or something affecting the individual directly, and subsequently his relationship with the group. In either case he lost his place as a member of the team; alone now, he was overwhelmed and became disorganized'.[12]

In traditional war, the group provided the most important basis for the subject's psychic stability as well as for his motivation to fight.[13] Some military theorists thus conclude that:

> The men were motivated to fight not by ideology or hate, but by regard to their comrades, respect for their leaders, concern for their own reputation with both, and an urge to contribute to the success of the group. In return, the group provided structure and meaning to an otherwise alien existence, a haven from an impersonal process apparently intent on grinding the life from all involved.[14]

This group relationship very much involves the desire of the Other. The soldier thus identifies with what kind of an object he is supposed to be for the desire of the Other when he questions his role in the group.[15]

At the time of the Gulf War, a soldier who panicked before the future combat would often be counselled by his superiors that he is part of something important, so that he starts to identify with the organization that is bigger than himself: 'People in the organization become important to him. And it is more important for him not to fail them.' At the same time, a chaplain might convince him that 'it's an important aspect of obedience to God to keep your promise, keep your covenant, keep your oath (to defend the country).'[16] After the Vietnam War, prisoners of war reported that what sustained them in difficult situations was not only ideals like loyalty to the country, but especially an idealization of the family. They were very much concerned with the question of how the family would regard them when they came home, i.e. would they be worthy of their respect or not? And those who broke down under pressure, often got some relief for their guilt that others had broken down, too.[17]

Still another way of coping with an anxiety-provoking war situation is to imagine a danger that might befall one's family. Some soldiers who were waiting on the ships before being engaged in the Gulf War created an image of a family problem, which 'is as ominous as his impotence to deal with the problem'.[18] The concern for family welfare that he feels he cannot solve thus becomes a way for the soldier to deal with his own helplessness in regard to the unknown danger that might await him in combat.

Military psychiatry heavily relies on the knowledge that anxiety is related to the question of the desire of the Other. For example, studies have shown that the soldier who has suffered breakdown is best treated near the battlefront where he is close to his comrades and that soldiers who are removed from the war zone or sent back home take longer to recover.

Paradoxically, the Soviet army in the Second World War, which kept its soldiers at the front no matter what and did not acknowledge psychological breakdown as an excuse for withdrawing from the battle, suffered a smaller number of long-term psychiatric casualties than other armies, which tended to send the troubled soldiers out of the war zone.[19]

Military psychiatry still considered group relations as most important for the soldier's endurance of the war-situation during the Second World War, but by the time of the wars in Korea and in Vietnam the military preferred to embrace the idea of individualism. The soldier was thus trained as an individual who could be placed into a group for a short time, quickly removed from it if necessary, or posted to another one. During the Korean War, psychiatrists started talking about the 'short-termer's syndrome' and 'rotation anxiety' when they were describing the psychological problems of soldiers as, with the disruption of group support, combat became an individual struggle and the short-term soldier felt very much disengaged from his comrades. Similarly, in Vietnam, psychiatry used the term 'disorder of loneliness' for describing states of apathy, defiance or violent behaviour that emerged among the soldiers on the battlefield.[20] The military there used a twelve-month rotation system, which meant that individual soldiers were injected into a war zone as individual replacements and then after a year were also individually extracted – often they were deposited back into the normal life as civilians a mere twenty-four hours after they left base camp.[21] The Vietnam veterans also encountered enormous public antipathy in their hometowns, which removed the likelihood of them receiving any kind of moral 'repayment' for their actions by the absence of an acknowledgement that their actions were for the public good.[22]

Similar problems occurred with soldiers who served as peacekeepers in Bosnia, where the Canadian media reported that their troops suffered from numerous attacks of anxiety and depression when they returned from the front. Wendy Holden points out that peacekeepers suffer from the fact that they must observe atrocities, but are helpless to fight back or to defend properly those they have been sent to save: 'Proud to become professional soldiers and keen to fight a war, they are, however, distanced from death and the reality of killing. They are members of a society that finds fatalities unimaginable. When presented with the unimaginable, they crack.'[23] British peacekeeper Gary Bohanna came to Bosnia with the belief that a peacekeeping role is supposed to be good, better in any case than a role in a war in which colleagues get killed. But he quickly became disillusioned when he saw numerous civilians killed, women being raped, whole families slaughtered. For him the most traumatic event, the one which precipitated his breakdown, was when he saw a young girl who, as he depicts her, '[had] shrapnel wounds in her head, half her head was blown away. Her eye was coming out of its socket and she was screaming. She was going to die, but I couldn't bear her pain. I put a blanket over her head and shot her in her head. That was all I could do.'[24] Here again we find a case of a soldier who comes to the war with the protective shield of a fantasy: this time it is a fantasy that he is actually coming to do good deeds and is not fully entering the war. However, this fantasy quickly collapses when something happens that undermines the story he was telling himself beforehand.

MOURNING AND SUICIDE

Many veterans fall into depression after the wars in which they have served, and sometimes also experience anxiety attacks. These traumas can bring the sufferer even to the point of suicide. One veteran describes his suffering in the following words:

> I usually feel depressed. I've felt this way for years. There have been times I've been so depressed that I won't even leave the basement. I'll usually start drinking pretty heavily around these times. I've also thought about committing suicide when I've been depressed. I've got an old .38 that I snuck back from Nam. A couple of times I've sat with it loaded, once I even had the barrel in my mouth and the hammer pulled back. I couldn't do it. I see Smitty back in Nam with his brains smeared all over the bunker. Hell, I fought too hard then to make it back to the World [the US]: I can't waste it now. How come I survived and he didn't? There has to be some reason.[25]

To understand these self-destructive tendencies, we need to go back to Freud's discussion of anxiety. When Freud took anxiety as a reaction to the danger of the loss of an object, he posed the question: What is the difference between anxiety and other types of reaction to the loss of the object, like mourning and melancholy? Mourning is the process of the separation from the object, which no longer exists. This process of separation in mourning occurs under the influence of reality testing, which requires the bereaved person to undo the ties that bind him or her to the object. Through mourning the subject is able to detach him- or herself from the lost object, i.e. accept its loss, whereas in melancholy the subject insists in the narcissistic identification with the lost object; in anxiety, however, the subject reacts to the very danger resulting from the loss of the object. Thus, anxiety and melancholy are two different reactions to the loss of the object, which paradoxically seem to complement each other, since anxiety signals a danger over the loss of the object, whereas melancholy appears as a solution to this, as the subject insists in identification with the lost object.

Lacan agreed with Freud that anxiety is the subject's response to the threat of castration. As such, in the formation of the subject, anxiety needs to be taken as something that precedes the formation of desire. When the subject becomes a speaking being, language marks the subject and deprives him or her of some essential *jouissance*.[26] The subject, for example, will thus not have any sexual drive toward a member of the opposite sex in order to ensure the reproduction of the species. Enjoyment for the subject will often seem as something lost, something inaccessible, or something stolen by others. If the process of symbolic castration (i.e. entering into language) extracts *jouissance* from the body, leaving it only in the margins of partial drives, then anxiety later becomes an excitation, which aims at this lost *jouissance*. Paradoxically, anxiety thus becomes a median between desire and *jouissance*. As such, anxiety appears to the subject as something that is beyond doubt or uncertainty – as some kind of a signal of the real beyond the symbolic in which the subject operates as a speaking being.

This explanation complicates the question of the nature of mourning and the nature of melancholy. Lacan makes a puzzling statement, which suggests that the object we are mourning was the unknowing support of our castration. When the subject becomes a speaking being, the subject experiences a loss, which will never be filled. However, the subject often tries to deal with the loss of the object, which concerns both the lack that marks the subject and the lack that marks the Other, by presenting him- or herself as what is lacking to the

Other. That is why when we mourn the loss of someone we mourn him or her because we perceived ourselves to be his or her lack.[27] Perceiving oneself to be the object of the desire of the Other is in the final analysis one of the ways in which the subject deals with the fact that he or she is marked by lack.

In contrast to a mourning subject, the melancholic confuses loss and lack. The main characteristic of the object cause of desire is that it is always already lacking, i.e. that it is another name for the lack itself. The melancholic however perceives the *lack* of the object as a *loss* of the object. He or she behaves as if at some point in the past the object was found and now it is lost. For Lacan, melancholy is therefore a particular solution that the subject gives to castration wherein, by continuing to identify with the lost object, the subject also forms a particular form of desire and *jouissance*. The melancholic who seems to abolish desire, on the one hand finds precisely in this state of 'giving up' a particular form of desire (as similarly does an anorexic), and on the other hand finds also a particular form of *jouissance*.

A soldier who falls into a deep melancholy after serving in a war and continuously asks himself why he was spared death while his colleague was not, deals in a particular way with his dilemma with lack. In his melancholic withdrawal from the world or by immersion in alcohol he finds a painful form of *jouissance*, which he is often not willing to give up. However, as well as dealing with his lack, he also deals with the lack in the Other, since he often questions what kind of an object he was for the Other – for example, what he meant to another colleague or what he meant for the big Other (e.g. society at large). The search for recognition from society or the family thus becomes extremely important. And, it is this desire (desire for recognition and thus a temporal solution to the lack that marks the subject) which can help us explain the military need for decorating veterans with various insignias. In some instances loss of such recognition has precipitated the suicide of a veteran.

One such (surprising) case concerned a suicide in the mid 1990s. Admiral Jeremy M. Boorda, a former Vietnam Veteran and a top US Navy Officer in the Bosnian war, put a bullet into his head after being questioned whether he truly earned two Vietnam-era decorations which he wore on his uniform. Admiral Boorda liked to decorate himself with V-shaped pins, which were given to individuals who were exposed to personal hazards due to direct hostile action. A journalist for *Newsweek Magazine* started investigating whether Boorda truly earned those pins, and after the meeting with the journalist Boorda killed himself. In a farewell note, Boorda explained that he simply could not live with the disgrace that the exposure of the truth about his insignia would bring to him. This case shows the importance of the symbolic insignias that soldiers receive after a war. It is as if their whole identity relies on a couple of pins with which they decorate their uniforms. However, it is interesting that Boorda pretended to be honoured for his involvement in the most hazardous military actions. His need to decorate himself with pins he did not truly earn shows how Boorda centred his self-perception on the idea that he survived an enormous danger. And at the moment when he would have been exposed in his cheating, he decided to kill himself.

After the war, one mostly encounters two types of suicide. First are those linked to the emergence of trauma after an anxiety-provoking event. In these cases it looks as if the soldiers were never able to recompose themselves after their individual fantasy structures were shattered. Soldiers who were severely traumatized after an anxiety-provoking event often did not want to use their suicide as a means of calling to the Other by the writing of suicide notes. This is rather what Lacan calls a *passage à l'acte*, an act of self-annihilation of the subject, which does not try to incite a response from the Other. The second common type of suicide that one encounters among war veterans is similar to that of Admiral Boorda. These suicides are related to the problem of honour and respect. The war veterans often feel that they did not get a proper symbolic recognition for their suffering in war and their suicide might be a last desperate attempt to receive a response from the Other. That is why such veterans write a note in which they explain their action hoping that the Other will finally recognize them. These suicides are more an acting-out than a *passage à l'acte* since the veterans still have a firm belief in the big Other.

An example of a veteran whose suicide is an attempt to get a response from the Other is evident in the case of Vu Quang So who, more than thirty years after the war, burned himself alive in front of the police headquarters in southern Vietnam. Such acts of self-immolation were practised in the early 1960s as forms of protest by the Buddhist monks against the Ngo Dinh Diem regime in Saigon. When Vu Quang So performed such self-sacrifice, some tried to find an explanation in the traumas that he suffered as a result of the war, while others claimed that his desperate act was a protest against the way the regime was treating the veterans. So's military pension was inadequate to support himself and his family so that as a result he was forced to sell ice cream to earn his living. He was apparently driven to the suicidal act after a dispute with the police over his right to sell ice cream on the street. When he was told that he needed to pay a fine for his confiscated stall, he returned to the police station with a bottle of gasoline, poured it over himself, and struck a match to his clothes.

Lacan observes that in cases when people commit suicide by jumping through a window, the window might be perceived as the window of fantasy. The subject self-annihilates himself because his fantasy has collapsed – he thus seems to be literally jumping out of his fantasy. In the case of the man who burned himself alive in front of the police building, however, we do not find the same type of self-annihilation. Here, the subject is much more concerned to send a message to the authorities, i.e. the subject tries to provoke the big Other to recognize his suffering.

FANTASY OF BAYONET KILLING

Since fantasy protects the subject from anxiety, military psychiatry in the past tried to use the power of fantasy to incite soldiers to engage in combat; the anti-Nazi allies, for example, tried to artificially create fantasies that would help soldiers overcome their initial reluctance to kill. This need for psychological training in aggression was especially strengthened when a military theorist, Colonel S. L. A. Marshall, reported that almost three-quarters of the soldiers were unwilling to kill in combat. This figure was later proclaimed fake, but it nonetheless determined the perception that psychology was needed to incite aggression in combatants. In the early 1940s the British army, for example, introduced special 'blood training' and 'battle schools': animals' blood was squirted on to faces during bayonet drill; men were taken to slaughterhouses and encouraged to test the 'resistance of a body' by using their 'killing knives' on the carcasses; and 'kill that Hun . . . kill that Hun' was chanted from the loudspeakers as soldiers waded through water and mud pits, were shot at with live ammunition, and fired their own weapons at three-dimensional imitation Germans and Japanese.[28]

To teach soldiers how to kill and to motivate them to do so, it was thus important to create an artificial fantasy scenario, i.e. killing was presented in the light of a story with which the soldiers might have been able to identify. One possible scenario was to present killing as a hunt on animals, as we see in an Australian training instruction pamphlet: 'The enemy is the game, we the hunters. The Jap is a barbarian, little better than an animal, in fact his actions are those of a wild beast and he must, therefore, be dealt with accordingly.'[29] This training tried to incite the subject's inner aggression and to control his anxiety and guilt. Some of the trainers who were influenced by psychoanalysis also tried to present the killing of the enemy as a mythical rite in which the death of the leader of the enemy group is celebrated in 'an orgy of displaced violence', since this slaughter satisfies

> deep-seated, primitive unconscious strivings derived from early childhood fantasy. . . . The enemy is a sacrificial object whose death provides deep group satisfaction in which guilt is excluded by group sanction. Combat is a ritualistic event, which resolves the precarious tension of hatred created by the long drawn frustrations of training. Without these frustrations, a group would not be a military force.[30]

Here we thus have an incentive to recreate in reality the Freudian theory of the killing of the primal father (in the guise of the enemy leader) and the establishment of strong brotherly bonds among the soldiers.

While military psychologists tried artificially to create fantasies with which the soldiers would identify, soldiers themselves actually created their own fantasies, and in their diaries, for example, often reported killing someone with a bayonet and how the victim just before dying looked into the attacker's eyes with dismay, as if shocked to see the killer's identity. This memory of being recognized by the victim is quite common among soldiers; however, military statistics show that the bayonet is rarely used in war and that most killing is done from a distance where the attacker remains anonymous for the victim. It is thus obvious that the memory of bayonet killing is in most cases a fantasy, a scenario produced by the soldier himself. This fantasy is obviously extremely valuable, since even in contemporary army, where one cannot expect many one-to-one battles, the soldiers are still extensively trained in bayonet killing. However, even in the First World War, military instructors already had great difficulty teaching soldiers how to properly use the bayonet. Most soldiers had the idea that they needed to toss a bayoneted enemy over their shoulder, and many accounts of combat in popular literature depicted scenes in which a soldier bayonets an enemy and hurls him over his shoulder 'just as a man might toss a bundle of hay with a pitchfork'.[31]

While soldiers claimed they prefered bayonet killing to anonymous killing because it is more personal and their responsibility is clear, military psychologists were trying to convince soldiers that war is just an impersonal game in which they are not responsible for their actions since they sacrifice themselves for a higher cause. The paradox is that the soldiers responded to this explanation by creating their own fantasies of killing. In the memories of the bayonet killing that never took place it is crucial that the enemy recognizes the killer with his shocked gaze, but by pitchforking the enemy, the killer then tries to quickly get rid of this gaze. This example shows that the soldiers also did not want to give up the guilt for their actions, for although military psychologists were trying to convince them that they were not responsible for their killing, the soldiers insisted on their guilt to the point of inventing crimes they never committed.

ANXIETY-FREE WARS

If in the two World Wars there was still some minimal engagement with victims on the battlefield, in recent wars the soldier is often just a distant actor who shoots from afar and does not even know what happens on the actual front. Contemporary wars are supposed to be aseptic, so that American soldiers might fly for a couple of hours to drop bombs over Afghanistan and then return home to watch the soccer game on TV. For those soldiers still required to engage in direct fighting, military psychiatry is trying to invent some special medication to alleviate any possible anxiety.[32] The soldiers will thus be almost robot-like creatures who will not be emotionally engaged in the atrocities they are committing. One theory why it is necessary to invent such drugs is that war's reality has become too horrible for the human mind and body to tolerate.[33] Military psychiatry therefore has an expectation that in the new types of war anxiety will be just too overwhelming and paralysing – hence their attempts to find a chemical substance, which will alleviate it.[34] So far all the attempts to create such drugs have been unsuccessful, and anti-anxiety drugs used on the front not only failed to alleviate anxiety, but also produced numerous side effects, which reduced soldiers to zombie-like creatures, barely able to function or perform their duties.

The history of wars is, of course, full of accounts about which substances helped the soldiers to endure the stresses of the battles, and drugs and alcohol have always been part of the soldier's life. However, today Western armies conduct most of their operations at night, which requires use of drugs that help the soldier to stay awake for many nights.[35] Since wars also incite many traumas and feelings of guilt, the next hopeful invention will attempt to address and alleviate this. The fantasy drug of the future will be able to erase in the mind of the soldier any memory of the traumatic situation. So far research that has been done on rats indicates that 'the brain's hormonal reactions to fear can be inhibited, softening the formation of memories and the emotions they evoke'.[36] While some researchers try to tackle fear and guilt by decoding the gene behind a fear-inhibiting protein, others are trying to figure out how to help the brain unlearn fear by stimulating it with magnets, and still others are examining what happens with survivors of car accidents if they take propranol pills, which are supposed to nip the effects of trauma in the bud.[37]

The ultimate fantasy drug would act as some kind of morning-after pill that would affect the centres in the brain where traumatic memory is stored, so that after a horrible experience a person would not suffer from regret, remorse, pain or guilt. Often research into such drugs is inspired by the idea that if a way of erasing traumatic memory could be found it would be of great help to rape victims. However, many are afraid that such drugs primarily would be exploited by the military and brand such future medicine 'devil' or 'monster' pills. Since such drugs would also radically affect our perception of what is right and what is wrong, some are calling them also 'anti-morality' pills. Critics are questioning whether we are ready for the fact that pharmaceuticals will enable soldiers to rely on the infamous Nuremberg plea – 'I was just following orders.'

Psychotherapists are also testing ways of alleviating the suffering of those experiencing anxiety and traumas after participating in war with the help of the so-called virtual clinic. The idea of these clinics is that the patient who for example suffers trauma related to his engagement in a war situation is given at the clinic the opportunity of reliving the traumatic situation and thus becoming desensitized to it. The patient must wear special glasses, which function like a projection screen showing images from the war. The patient thus hears noises from the battlefield, sees helicopters flying, etc. The virtual clinic is based on the idea that the subject's anxiety can be successfully annihilated if he or she is able to consciously re-experience the traumatic situation and that continuous exposure to it will supposedly alleviate the anxiety-provoking activity. However, as Freud has already pointed out with regard to the war neuroses of his own time, the emergence of anxiety or other neurotic symptoms in the war or post-war situation is never simply linked to the presence of objective danger, but to the subject's unconscious. Which is why anxieties that the soldiers experience in regard to their participation in war are not so different from other types of anxieties, since anxiety always has to do with the subject's problem with the threat of castration.

If military psychiatry in the past hoped to incite fantasies that would encourage soldiers to kill, today's virtual clinics have the idea that simple behaviour changes (and some medication) can alter the subject's psyche. This attempt to find quick solutions for the subject's anxieties is not an isolated phenomenon. It looks as if in general we are living in a society in which subjects are supposed to suffer no anxieties anymore – especially no anxieties with regard to death.

ARTS AND DEATH

What kind of society will this be in which the subjects are supposed to suffer no anxiety anymore when they are observing destruction on the battle front or when they are engaged in violence? Paradoxically, some trends in today's art scene can give us clues about the changes in contemporary society that give ground to the vision of an anxiety-free future society.

After the age of anxiety that emerged after the First World War, in the midst of despair and bitterness emerged a new modernist movement since, as Hans Arp, one of the establishers of Dadaism noted, people lost interest in the slaughter-houses of the world. While Dada tried to show the absurdities of life, surrealism found insights in psychoanalysis and tried to look beyond the tyranny of reason into the domain of the fantasies and dreams of the unconscious. Some new forms of art were experimenting with the unknown, abandoning tradition, and others were exposing the dark side of the values of Western civilization. For some artists suicide seemed the only response to the depression provoked by that valueless civilization.

If we look at the contemporary age of anxiety, here, too, the art scene seems in a particular way to react to the crisis.[38] In the 1990s the arts on the one hand very much tried to show everyday life as an art object, while on the other hand to depict what lay behind things – for example, the inside of the body. It looked as if everything could be exposed and that there is nothing to surprise us in what is supposed to be behind the mask. And, just as in the case of war we were able to see all kinds of suffering exposed on the screen, the bodies being torn in front of our eyes,[39] people killing each other and even recording their acts with the video camera, so in the arts we had a similar trend – it seemed as if every act of violence concerning the body could be presented as an art work. These trends have been predominant precisely in the famous show Sensation. The exposure of what is supposed to be the hidden inside can be seen in Damien Hirst's split animals, Monna Hatum's video of the intestines, Alain Miller's picture of the face behind the skin, Mark Quinn's skin without the body, Ron Mueck's *Dead Dad*, and even Chris Ofili's use of animal excreta. On the other hand, we have depiction of everyday life in the work of Tracey Emin's exposure of the names of all her lovers, Sara Lucas's mattress, etc.

One can also find examples of the exposure of the inside (i.e. of what was hidden) in some architecture. If one looks at the design of many new restaurants, one can see that the work process is supposed to be totally exposed to the public. Everywhere, one now finds restaurants which look like factories – when one walks in, one sees low-paid workers preparing the food, washing the dishes, etc. We observe these workers as decorative art objects and do not think about the hardship that these people might endure or how uncomfortable they might feel about being exposed as if in a zoo.

Still other examples of this logic of 'exposing the secret' can be found in today's election campaigns. Politicians in their TV advertisements have stopped delivering the final product – a speech that is supposed to convince the electorate – so that, often, the advertisement exposes the very preparation of the speech. We might see a politician who shaves himself in the bathroom, sips his morning coffee, talks to the advisers who are preparing his speech, etc. Where in the past, a politician would have hidden the fact that it is not he who writes the speech, today this very revelation is used as a campaign advertisement. The message that this advertisement puts across is: we show you the truth, the politician is just an ordinary man like you, and he is very honest, since he even shows you how he is not even writing his own speeches, etc.

In the 1990s the dominant ideology in the West was that there is no social antagonism in society anymore, i.e. that there is no lack. There seemed to be nothing secret, and the logic of 'showing everything' at first appeared as a way of alleviating anxiety by exposing what might be horrifying for the subject. In this context, the fear of death also seemed to have taken a new course.

In the war situation, death was presented in many different ways. On the one hand the deaths of 'enemies' became in the Western media either a mere question of numbers, or as something that can be exposed to the public, while the deaths and sacrifice of the Western soldiers appeared as extremely traumatic. And the fact that today's wars are conducted mostly from a distance also opened up for the soldiers the possibility of taking their own dying at the front as something unimaginable.

Concerning these new dilemmas with regard to dying, art can again offer us an insight. Throughout history art has been concerned in a particular way with the issues of mortality and immortality. It is not only that artists have often reflected on these topics in their work, they also hoped that their own artistic creations would achieve some kind of immortality for themselves. While artists in former times wished to be symbolically present after their death, some artists in recent decades have actually tried to devise ways of preserving their bodies after death. Orlan, Stelarc and Marcelli Antunez Roca, for example, plan to use new computer technologies in different ways to achieve immortality. Orlan developed an idea that after her death her body should be mummified and placed in an art gallery; and with the help of a computer device the visitors will be able to communicate with her in eternity. Stelarc has been for many years trying to create a new meta-body in which the organs become replaceable, the skin more durable, and the body starts acting without expectation, produces movements without memory, has no desires, etc. For this new body there will be no burden to deal either with birth or with death: reproduction will be substituted by redesigning and sexual intercourse replaced with the interface between the subject and the machine. And Marcelli Antunez Roca created a robot that can be moved with the help of sensors navigated by visitors to the gallery: after his death this robot will become his prosthesis through which the artist will continue to be alive.

These artists played with the idea that new computer technology can allow us to create an immortal body. But with the new developments in genetic science and medicine, there has also been a major shift in the arts. A number of artists are now exploring how the new knowledge about the genes alters human life, while others reflect on the issues of life and death by using real cadavers in their art projects. A couple of years ago, Britain was shocked when it was discovered that the artist Anthony-Noel Kelly moulded his sculptures from the parts of cadavers he transported by subway from the local morgue. Although the artist claimed that he had no morbid fascination with the dead but only found beauty in anatomy and wanted to 'de-mystify' death, the court sent him to prison for his act. Artist/scientist Günter von Hagens also attracts huge crowds to see more than 200 so-called plastinates, i.e. specially prepared human corpses. At this exhibition one can see the inside of every single body organ and even observe a dead pregnant woman cut open.

There are other artists too who use cadavers or parts of them in their artistic creations. Joel-Peter Witkin, for example, became well known for his special type of photography, which depicts dead and disabled bodies. Some time ago, we could see in the Škuc Gallery in Ljubljana the work of the Ukrainian artist Ilya Chichkin who reflected on the Chernobyl catastrophe by decorating images of dead foetuses with pieces of jewellery. And Richard Shannabrook became known for his chocolate pralines, which are moulded on the scars of the dead people he found in a morgue.

The actual experience of dying itself became appropriated as artistic experience. Thus, Bill Viola exhibited moments of birth and dying as part of video installation; at the Manifesta show in Ljubljana, a film pictured a woman in the act of strangling herself; and Slovene body artist Ive Tabor liked to explore the whereabouts of the line between life and death by stopping his heart by putting a catheter through his veins. Franco B. became famous by letting his blood drip from his veins in the art gallery to the point of collapse, and at the opening of the 'Body and the East' art show in New York a Croatian performance artist decided to drink huge quantities of alcohol, which might easily have killed him.

Our ancestors might well have had a hard time understanding why robots or other types of new media machinery are art objects, or what is artistic in the use of a real cadaver in an exhibition, but in today's society the logic of what art represents has radically changed. Modernism still tried to depict the invisible, give it form and make it accessible to our perception; abstract art dealt with the issue of how to depict the very lack or absence of the object; but contemporary art has a different approach to the unrepresentable, i.e. to the lack as such. We can sketch this difference by looking at the depiction of the female genitals. Gustave Courbet is most known for his painting, *L'origine du monde* that shows the exposed female genitals which, in classical paintings, are usually covered by fig leaves. As is well known, this picture has been for a long time in the possession of Jacques Lacan. The latter, however, did not expose it in its full nudity, but asked Andre Masson to paint an abstract picture of a forest-like stylized image, which was then placed on top of Courbet's painting. These two pictures show in a paradoxical way the difference in how realist and abstract art deal with the lack, i.e. with the traumatic, invisible, beautiful and horrifying thing that is, for example, associated with female genitals. If Courbet's realism tries to depict this lack by making the object (the female genitals) as real as possible, Masson's abstract painting shows the very absence of the object. The stylized forest might allude to the pubic hair, but it also shows that the sublime object (the female genitals) is something utterly absent – i.e. it is nothing but a lack. In today's art, however, we have a different approach towards lack.

Mona Hattum and Stelarc have in their art works used micro-cameras to show what the inside of the colon looks like; and Slovenian philosopher/artist Peter Mlakar has done the same with the vagina in his very interesting performance about the 'G-spot'. However, all these attempts to use new technologies to expose what is supposed to be invisible, actually do not depict lack as lack, but involve a certain denial of the lack, just as the picture of the genetic structure or even its scientific decoding does not give us a clue as to what constitutes the essence of the human being. Similarly, art which indulges in revealing everything that is supposed to be invisible, ungraspable or horrifying does not alleviate anxiety that people might have with regard to their bodies. Seeing the inside of the colon or vagina might make us shocked at how unromantic the inside looks, yet in no way affect sexual fantasies, hypochondriac fears, sublime attraction or disgust with regard to what is the ungraspable in the body. As Freud and Lacan already thought decades ago, the perception of the human body has very little to do with anatomy and is in fact all to do with language, fantasies and the unconscious. A real cadaver in an art project might be understood as a shocking device with which the artist tries to get closer to the traumatic point of death and be better able to expose its horrifying nature. But a paradoxical feature of the dead bodies that are used in art is that they are in some way perceived as undead – though not as some kind of living dead, like the vampires or spectres who return and haunt the living.

While wars are using ever more sophisticated weapons and there seems to be increasing danger of new conflicts emerging all around the globe, the development of science and the waste cyber-world of new technologies at the same time incite the impression that life is like a computer game and that we live in a world of simulacra in which bodies and identities are something we can change and play with. In this context the boundary between life and death also seems to have been changed. In cyberspace, one can enjoy playing with numerous imaginary personas; in the near future it will be possible to create new body-parts out of existing genetic material, and it is easy to envision that new genetic technologies will at some point allow the laboratory production of the whole human body. In this context, the Western soldier equipped with new sophisticated weapons also appears more and more immortal.

Fantasy and anxiety present two different ways for the subject to deal with the lack that marks him or her as well as the Other, i.e. the symbolic order. With the help of the fantasy, the subject creates a story, which gives his or her life a perception of consistency and stability, while he or she also perceives the social order as being coherent and not marked by antagonisms. If fantasy provides a certain comfort to the subject, anxiety incites the feeling of being uncomfortable. However, anxiety does not simply have a paralysing effect. The power of anxiety is that it creates a state of preparedness, so that the subject might be less paralysed and surprised by events that might radically shatter his or her fantasy and thus cause the subject's breakdown or the emergence of a trauma.

In today's society we have attempts to create a situation in which, on the one hand, the subject's anxieties will possibly be eliminated (for example, with the help of drugs that the military is trying to invent) and, on the other hand, to make everything visible so that there will be nothing to be anxious about anymore. But while ideology presents how everything is visible in contemporary society, people are nonetheless constantly left with the impression that someone else is running the show behind their backs or that there is a hidden enemy who has to be exposed and eliminated. For example, the military's attempts to find drugs that would alleviate anxiety on the battlefront, instead of preventing the soldiers' anxieties, are actually helping to generate new ones. It is unclear how much the military has actually tested drugs on the battlefield (for example, at the time of the Gulf War[40]), but soldiers have indulged in numerous conspiracy theories: a whole set of new anxieties is emerging with regard both to the scientists who are supposedly testing dangerous drugs on the soldiers and also to the paralysing side effects these drugs have.[41] The ultimate trauma for the soldiers thus becomes to fight the hidden enemy among those who have sent them to war in the first place.

Today it looks as if we live in a world of simulacra in which everything is changeable and in which life looks like a computer game. People thus have a perception that with a proper genetic code and the invention of new drugs matters of life and death will be more predictable and controllable in the future. But maybe the perception that today's world is so radically different from the old one because of the advances in modern technology is the ultimate fantasy which protects us, first, from the fact that the subject (i.e. the individual) is still fully marked by a lack and that the social (i.e. society) is still marked by antagonisms. Although people might have the impression that they can now predict, prevent or at least fully describe the disturbing objects that emerge at the place of the lack, they are actually not alleviating anxiety. One can even claim that science creates ever-new ones. Genes today become an especial source of anxiety. Since human genes continue to be 'alive' after the subject's death, the human body more and more appears as non-destroyable. However, with these attempts to further master death, we should not forget the famous prediction of Kierkegaard that for the subject more horrible than death is actually the possibility of immortality.

Three

When we are told that we live in the new age of anxiety, our first impression is perhaps that this is related to the proliferation of possible catastrophes such as terrorist attacks, the collapse of the financial market, strange illnesses, ecological changes, the threat of new wars and new developments in science. However, it is in fact arrogant to claim that our civilization experiences more anxieties than that of our predecessors, for they too had to deal with wars and conflicts, poverty, and many more illnesses that radically shortened people's lives. Nevertheless, although anxieties relating to possible catastrophes might not be so very different today from those of the past, the anxieties that particulary relate to contemporary society are linked to new feelings of insecurity, stemming from the nature of contemporary capitalism, for although insecurities have always been the vehicle of the capitalist labour market, in post-industrial society we can observe changes in the subject's self-perception that have in turn been affected by the transformations in the social symbolic order.

Consumerist society seems to thrive on a particular feeling of inadequacy that people commonly experience today. To grasp the power of this feeling we need only look at any women's magazine or the 'style' section of a daily newspaper.

What we find in such publications, apart from advertising and reports on the latest fashion, cosmetics and celebrities, is advice. We live in times characterized by survival. Therefore it is not untypical to come across articles on subjects such as the single girl's guide to survival; a mother's secret diary on how to survive childbirth (since 'having babies does terrible damage, especially to the fashionably fortyish mother'); advice on how to survive being in or out of a relationship; advice on diet and exercise, etc. Of course, such advice radically changes over time, so that, as one typical column claims, until recently 'we have become neurotic about getting enough sleep, but the new research now suggests that the less we have, the longer we'll live'.[1]

In sum, such magazines offer a cocktail of advice and prohibitions that ends up tasting of guilt. If the ideology of the 1990s followed the commands 'Just do it!' and 'Be yourself!'[2] today it seems that the new motto the media promotes is: 'No matter what you do, you will do it wrong, but it is better that you follow our advice and try again.' The 'Just do it!' ideology relied on the idea that the subject is 'free' in the sense of being a non-believer in authority and a person capable of changing his or her identity at will. Today it looks as if we are living in times when people have woken up and acknowledged their limitations in such pursuits. However, it is not so much that we have finally realized that we are not self-creators, who can reject old authorities like religion or the state and make out of ourselves a work of art unfettered by any cultural or even biological restraints; it is rather that the very ideology of 'Just do it!' instead of offering unlimited optimism opened the doors to a particular anxiety. This anxiety is linked to the very idea that we now have freedom to create an image in which we will appear likeable to ourselves, since today more people than ever before experience all kinds of traumas related to their body image, and as a result are suffering from anorexia, bulimia, excessive exercising, obsession with plastic surgery, and shopping addiction. What is so horrifying in the very possibility of making out of oneself a work of art, i.e. of being free to create our lives the way we want to? Why does the very freedom that we supposedly have for making choices in our lives account for an increase of anxiety?

ANXIETY BETWEEN DESIRE AND *JOUISSANCE*

Freud speculated that anxiety in adulthood is linked to guilt, which is why anxiety has an important connection with the superego. Lacan also stressed this connection and pointed out that the superego functions as the voice that commands the subject to enjoy yet at the same time mockingly predicts that he or she will fail in this pursuit of enjoyment. While it is easy to conclude that anxiety relates to this feeling of guilt linked to the superego's command, one could invert this concept and thus produce a fresh insight whereby, paradoxically, it is not the possibility of failure but rather the possibility of success which produces anxiety. Here we need to remember two well-known Lacanian points about anxiety, analysed in the previous chapter: first, that anxiety is not incited by the lack of the object but rather by the lack of the lack, i.e. the emergence of an object in the place of lack; and second, that anxiety is a median between desire and *jouissance*.

Desire is always linked to dissatisfaction (to the lack of the object), while *jouissance* brings the subject close to the object, often in most painful ways. When we say that desire is linked to lack, we should not be too quick to conclude either that there is never a proper object that can satisfy desire, or that success in failure is a particular strategy of the desiring subject who always complains that whatever he or she attained is not 'it'. The paradoxical feature of desire is that it is not some kind of an insatiable mouth that goes from one object to another and is never satisfied: desire itself is put in motion only when the subject encounters the object of desire, i.e. the Lacanian object *a*, which is another name for the lack itself. However the lack does not start existing when we come to an object of desire but rather when desire is replaced with *jouissance* – which is when we come close to an object that is no longer the elusive object of desire but rather the object that incites a particular enjoyment often coupled with pain, and thus horrifying for the subject.

In love relationships this might happen when a hysteric who has been longing for a particular partner finally has a successful sexual encounter with them, yet as a result is totally horrified by the experience and immediately abandons the partner. However, the problem may not be simply that the subject wants to keep his or her desire unsatisfied (i.e. to keep longing for the inaccessible object), but may rather be linked to coming too close to the object of *jouissance*. In this context, Lacan makes a comment that orgasm is a state of anxiety that the subject usually tolerates quite well; however, it can also be a point that the subject very much tries to avoid.

How, therefore, is anxiety linked to failure? And why does the subject often desperately try to prevent success? Anxiety is often perceived as a state of dissatisfaction, an excitation that the subject feels when he or she is not content with his or her life; but in light of psychoanalytic theory, this might not be the case, since anxiety is primarily an affect that warns us of the painful encounter with *jouissance*. Thus if one takes success not as a blissful state of harmony but as coming close to *jouissance*, anxiety can be perceived as a protective shield from *jouissance* which also allows desire to stay alive.

How therefore does today's capitalist ideology play on this anxiety? One can easily observe that the whole marketing system on which capitalism constantly relies engages the logic of desire and introduces the feeling that no matter what material goods we attain this is not 'it'. However, if we complicate this understanding of the logic of desire with the logic of *jouissance*, the way capitalism plays with anxiety gets new meaning.

When Kierkegaard[3] analysed anxiety, he took it to be something that is linked to possibility in existence. Here anxiety became specifically linked to freedom, or as Kierkegaard says, it is linked to freedom's actuality as the possibility of possibility. The subject who is free is therefore anxious precisely because of the indeterminacy, i.e. 'the possibility of possibility',[4] that freedom entails. That is why Kierkegaard concludes that anxiety is in the end anxiety before myself, which means that I am the sole arbiter and what I do is entirely up to me. Anxiety is thus linked to the possibility of being able, but, as such, it often appears as a feeling aroused by looking down into a yawning abyss.[5] Though Kierkegaard's speculations on anxiety might appear a world away from analysis of today's capitalism, it is possible to show that the popular debate about anxiety, with regard to the over-abundant choice that supposedly pertains to consumerist culture, very much follows the logic Kierkegaard had previously recognized.

How is this so-called abundance of choice[6] operative today? The last twenty years were dominated by the ideology that people would be happier and better off if they were constantly shopping for the best deals, so on the one hand, we got a huge emergence of new products, manufacturers and providers to choose from but, on the other hand, the idea of choice also became an end in itself. Some social scientists started to talk about the 'tyranny of freedom' in today's world, since consumers are forced to make choices even about things they never imagined they could have (or did not even want to have) any power over. An example here is the choice of electricity provider, which has incited considerable anxiety among consumers, since as a *New York Times* article explained, 'the anxiety over energy is exposing something even deeper in human wiring'.[7] It is not only that people do not want constantly to be perceived as autonomous, rational consumers: 'when it comes to electricity, a mysterious and dangerous thing that is also the foundation of modern living, Americans are just a little afraid to be alone.'[8] People are supposedly anxious for two reasons: first, it seems that no one is in charge in society anymore and, second, the freedom of choice actually does not give more power to the consumers, but to corporations. A person shopping around on the Internet for the best price for a product, for example, gives corporations a chance to collect valuable data about a consumer's desires and spending habits. What provokes anxiety for people therefore seems to be both that no one appears to be in control, and those who do exert control (the corporations) do so in hidden ways.

When people speak about anxiety today, they also invoke the idea that they are now asked to make choices about their sexuality, marriage and childbearing that used not to be regarded as choices in the past. But the more choices there are, the more it appears possible to achieve an ideal result in every case. This seems to be the case not only for people who are continually changing their long-distance telephone service in the hope of finding the best deal, but also for those searching for a love partner. If we look at the proliferation of self-help books devoted to love, it becomes clear that love is especially anxiety-provoking today and that people are searching for all kinds of guidance to alleviate this anxiety. In today's consumerist society, searching for a partner follows a similar logic to buying a new car: one first needs to do extensive research in the market; then check all the qualities of the desired 'object'; insure oneself with a pre-nuptial agreement; after some time exchange old for new or, in order to minimize the hassle, decide to go just for a short-term lease.

While on the one hand the Western subject is perceived to be a self-creator (i.e. a subject who can create out of him- or herself whatever he or she pleases, and who no longer relies on old authorities like family, religion and state), on the other hand the subject has lost the 'security' that the struggle with old authorities brought about. The shift that has happened in the subject's perception of him- or herself and his or her place in the social symbolic network, which incited new anxieties for subjects with regard to their body image and to their role in society at large, is very much linked to the way capitalism functions today. However, the ideology of consumerism is paradoxically also offering 'solutions' on how people should deal with this anxiety: it even seems that anxiety is the very motor of the marketing politics that dominate today's consumerist society.

ANXIETY AND THE NEW IMAGINARY

Psychoanalysis and marketing share the same knowledge that desire is always linked to prohibition. Freud was quite cynical about this fact and pointed out that where cultural prohibitions did not exist people invented them in order to keep desire alive,[9] and Lacan was quick to follow, stating that the subject would never want to have a sublime Thing unless the symbolic law were to prohibit access to it. With regard to consumer goods it is well known that we desire and cherish them more if they are expensive and hard to get. (I will never forget the enjoyment in the eyes of the Serbian student I met in Belgrade, who told me he obsessively cleans his one pair of Nike sneakers as he hopes to have them for a number of years.)

The new philosophy of the brand makers is that they do not try to prevent their logos being stolen and copied in the Third World. If a Turkish manufacturer, for example, makes copies of Nike sneakers, Nike will not try to prosecute him for copyright violation. Since Nike is primarily concerned with the dissemination of their logo, they take the fact that someone copied their product as just another advertising campaign. Another well-known strategy in creating 'addiction' to consumer goods is that Nike and similar brands like to throw their excess products into the poorest neighbourhoods, like the Bronx in New York City, and thus keep the young consumers attracted to their goods.[10]

If desire is linked to prohibition, does the fact that some companies nowadays give away products for free kill the desire? Paradoxically this does not happen, since today's capitalism does not simply rely on selling goods, but on the creation of a certain imaginary which people can identify with. In this context, the aforementioned feeling of inadequacy plays a strong role in the way marketing operates today. However, the problem is not that the media offer images of success and beauty with which people want to identify, and since they cannot come close to this ideal, they feel inadequate. For some time now the fashion industry, for example, has been convincing consumers that they should not follow fashion advice and try to make themselves into someone else, but should rather discover what is unique about themselves, and with the help of fashion just accentuate it. But, at the beginning of the last century, early attempts by the advertising industry to use psychoanalytic knowledge often relied on promoting an identification of the consumer with an authority. The advertisers' guess was that the consumer 'nearly always purchases in unconscious obedience to what he or she believes to be the dictates of an authority which is anxiously consulted or respected'.[11] In those days marketing thus tried to convince people to look and behave like someone else, i.e. to identify with an authority, whereas today, while people still look for role models (for example, in the entertainment industry), advertising is nonetheless much more playing with the idea that consumers will discover in such models 'heightened' aspects of themselves, and not simply follow the dictates of the market. However, this new marketing strategy creates a lot of unease for consumers, since what actually provokes anxiety in the subject is not the failure to be someone else, but an inability to be oneself.

In order to understand how anxiety is channelled in today's consumerism we need to first look at how capitalism works in contemporary Western societies. Numerous studies have recently analysed the change in capitalist production where, instead of material manufacturing being of foremost importance, the marketing of a particular image has become the main concern. In this new culture of capitalism, it is crucial that suppliers and users have replaced buyers and sellers; markets are managing pathways for networks and ownership is being replaced by access. Since the production costs of goods today are minimal and the market is so saturated with goods, the economy depends less on the individual market exchange of goods and more on the establishment of long-term commercial relationships.

For the companies the most important thing is the creation of a lifelong relationship with their customers in order that they may become their suppliers over a lifetime. Manufacturers thus invest most of their energy in developing trusting relations with their customers and trying to figure out what their future desires might be without the customers even being aware that they might actually want or need these things. Take, for example, the manufacturer of baby diapers who provides home delivery for its products: soon after the parents get the first delivery of the diapers, they start buying all other baby goods from this provider. As the baby grows up, the provider will then offer goods for toddlers and later adolescents. (One can easily imagine that the manufacturer might at some point also offer free psychoanalytic advice on how to raise children.)

As well as establishing a trusting relationship, contemporary manufacturers above all try to sell an image or, better, a lifestyle. Let us take the example of so-called 'designer coffees' sold at Starbucks or Coffee Republic. In these places what is sold is not simply coffee, but a particular type of experience: well-designed spaces, offering a cosy, homely atmosphere with a politically correct intellectual touch. One thus gets ecologically informed messages on how the coffee has been produced and even an explanation of how, by buying this (expensive) coffee, one helps the poor people in Colombia. On the one hand, the consumers of such expensive coffee are offered a symbolic space in which they appear likeable to themselves, but, on the other hand, they get protection from the outside world – especially from the poor.[12]

Today's capitalist society is making a long-term shift from industrial production to cultural production, in which cultural experiences are more important than goods and services. Jeremy Rifkin points out in his book *The Age of Access* that we are entering a so-called hyper-capitalism, or better 'cultural capitalism' that relies on the 'experience' economy[13] in which each person's own life becomes a commercial market:

> Global travel and tourism, theme cities and parks, destination entertainment centres, wellness, fashion and cuisine, professional sports and games, gambling, music, film, television, the virtual world of cyberspace, and electronically mediated entertainment of every kind are fast becoming the centre of a new hyper-capitalism that trades in access to cultural experience.[14]

In this context, businesses guess about a 'lifetime value' of their customers, trying to assess how much the latter are worth at every moment of their lives, and economists speak about the change that has happened from the commodification of space and material into the commodification of human time and duration. The prediction is that in the future almost everything will be a paid-for experience in which traditional reciprocal obligations and expectations – mediated by feelings of faith, empathy and solidarity – will be replaced by contractual relations in the form of paid memberships, subscriptions, admission charges, retainers and fees. The guess is that in the new era, people will purchase their very existence in small commercial segments, since their lives will be modelled on the movies so that 'each consumer's life experience will be commodified and transformed into an unending series of theatrical moments, dramatic events, and personal transformations'.[15]

Rifkin summarizes these new trends by pointing out that:

> In the new network economy what is really being bought and
> sold are ideas and images. The physical embodiment of these
> ideas and images becomes increasingly secondary to the
> economic process. If the industrial marketplace was
> characterized by the exchange of things, the network
> economy is characterized by access to concepts, carried
> inside physical forms.[16]

An example here again can be Nike, the company that truly
sells only image, and has no factories, machines or equipment, but only an extensive network of suppliers, so-called
production partners. Nike is merely a research and design
studio with a sophisticated marketing formula and distribution
system.

Another important point is that if what mattered in industrial society was the quantity of goods, in post-industrial
society this is replaced by quality of life, which is why we no
longer buy goods, but instead access them in time through,
for example, leasing and franchising. It looks as if capitalism is
losing its material origins and is becoming a temporal affair,
and this is linked to the fact that customers do not so much
need things, but just their function. In this context, the cus-
tomer becomes a client and partner who needs attention,
expertise and, most importantly, experience. (It is interesting
how psychoanalysis is also replacing the name patient with
client. And one wonders if some clients are doing analysis as
some kind of a new experience they want to buy.)

Still another crucial element in our new society is the
new evaluation of community, so that companies are desperate to create communities for their clients. In many companies' manuals one can thus read about the four stages for

dealing with clients: first, so-called 'awareness bonding', which makes the consumer aware of the new product or service; second, 'identity bonding' when the consumer starts in a particular way to identify with the brand; third, 'relationship bonding' when the consumer establishes a particular attachment to the brand; and fourth, 'community bonding' when the brand maker keeps consumers satisfied by organizing specific events and gatherings, or at least by sending birthday cards to the clients.

A particular marketing strategy that some brands of casual clothing use plays on an illusion of equality, which helps to mask class divides in today's world. Poorer consumers shop in outlets like Gap in order to appear middle class, while richer ones shop there in order to appear more 'ordinary'. Such brands also seem to erase gender difference in clothing, which changes the old divides in how men and women tend to choose their clothing. (As Darian Leader points out, women usually search for what no one else has, while men want to buy clothes that everyone else is wearing.)[17]

In sum, we are witnessing a transformation in the nature of commerce from the selling of things to the selling of images and creation of communities. The idea behind this change is that people above all want to appear likeable to others and to themselves and also want very much to 'belong'. Now that old types of communities (families, cultural groups) are in decline, by becoming subscribers, members, and clients, people acquire access to a new type of community. However, behind this attempt to create new communities is the perception that the totality of people's lived experience needs to be transformed into commercial fare. It looks as if human life itself becomes the ultimate commercial product. And some warn that when every aspect of our being becomes a paid-for activity then the commercial sphere becomes the final arbiter of our personal and collective existence.

If we introduce here the Lacanian concept of the Big Other, we can say that this search for the community can be understood as a search for a new Big Other and that the companies are playing precisely on this need on the part of the subject to have a perception of a coherent social symbolic order. But what is anxiety-provoking in this new play with images and new takes on community?

In Chapter Two, I pointed out how the questions that produce most anxiety in the subject involve the problem of how he or she appears in relation to the Other, in the meaning of another human being and the social symbolic network. Engagement with the Other can be traumatic for three different reasons: the subject might have problems with the Other's demand, with its desire, or with its *jouissance*. While the question of the Other's desire often comes formulated in the question: 'Who am I for the Other?' and the trauma of the Other's *jouissance* becomes perceived as the theft of our own *jouissance*, the problem that the subject has in regard to the Other's demand engages another logic. The subject often wants to get a demand from the Other and the horror emerges precisely when this demand is lacking, as, for example, in a psychoanalytic situation, where the analysand is perturbed by the lack of the demand coming from the analyst. Analysands hope to get clear instructions from the analyst, but instead get silence or questions that bounce their own problems back to them.

The problem with a society of 'too much choice' is that, on the one hand, there seems to be less and less demand coming from the Other and that the subject is much freer than in the past, while, on the other hand, the subject is constantly encouraged to pursue his or her own *jouissance*. We thus have a perception that we are now free from the old types of cultural and family constraints and that we can create an image of how we want ourselves to be and thus come close to a *jouissance* that we feel will bring us satisfaction. But although people in the developed world now have all this freedom and choice, they do not seem more content with their lives than their predecessors. Why does freedom of choice not bring us closer to happiness? One answer lies in the Lacanian description of *jouissance* as being something very much alien to ourselves (i.e. we do not 'choose' it in a rational way); which is why it is often when we are trying to be ourselves that we encounter something that is most traumatic and horrifying. The media create pressure on us to enjoy in the best possible way – to achieve the best possible orgasm, to be the best parent, spouse, worker, etc. The advice on how to come close to this *jouissance* then follows the logic expressed in one of the titles in *Cosmopolitan* magazine: 'Become yourself, only a better one.' But despite all this media advice on how one can become oneself there seems to be a lack of demand coming from the Other and the subject appears to be entirely free to find enjoyment that brings him or her satisfaction. As a result, the subject's anxiety increases because he or she has to face another demand in his or her inner self – the demand of the superego. Anxiety then becomes coupled with guilt.

THE HORROR OF POVERTY

The problem with theories that claim we live today in a form of cultural capitalism is that they neglect the fact that material production nonetheless continues, though often hidden in the countries of the Third World. Developed countries might have the perception that they are nowadays living in a virtual world of cultural capitalism, while most of their everyday products are made in China or by the invisible immigrant workers in the sweatshops of New York, sometimes the workers actually become visible, and are subsumed into the imaginary presented by the new type of capitalism as some kind of decorative art objects that offer proof of authenticity. In Chapter Two we pointed out how expensive restaurants with their open kitchens expose their low-paid workers to the public. We might think this decor is chosen as proof that cooking is really happening in the restaurant, to counter conspiracy theories like those that evolved around Chinese restaurants in Paris: the idea (a kind of urban myth) took hold there that the cooking was done in giant underground kitchens and when meals were ordered in a small, supposedly authentic restaurant, their chef just warmed up a pre-packed meal or ran to the underground kitchen to fetch it. However, one can also read this need to expose workers as decorative art objects as a particular way of tackling class divides today.

Recently there have been a number of books published in which middle-class writers decide to live for a period of time as poor workers, and in their books they depict the lives of the lower classes. Such books, of course, primarily try to prove that the liberal approach, which tries to replace welfare with 'workfare' is unsatisfactory, since people who earn minimal wages cannot make ends meet no matter how many hours they work per day. However, behind these attempts to show the impossibility of survival on minimal wages, one also finds an attempt to picture the lives of the poor in a way that calms the fears of the middle classes.

If a decade ago, the lower classes were primarily afraid for their jobs (or were permanently unemployed), now the same kind of insecurity touches the middle class. Ben Cheever in his memoir of a writer who becomes a low-paid salesman remembers a training course in the electronics store in which the teacher asked the future salesmen: 'What do people fear more than death?' 'Public speaking', was Cheever's answer.[18] This was definitely wrong, since the teacher reminded him that the greatest fear felt by Americans is that they will lose their job. And with the growing uncertainty about pension funds, people have also lost the belief in the possible security that will come in old age.

One way of tackling this insecurity is to observe the life of the poor in order to draw the conclusion: 'This is not me! I am far better off than they are.' Fran Abrams, the author of *Below the Breadline*, thus starts her book with the calming reassurance:

> Let me tell you about the nearly poor. They are, to misquote F. Scott Fitzgerald, different from you and me. They are soft where we are hard, cynical where we are trustful, in a way that unless you were born poor, it is very difficult to understand. They think, deep in their hearts, that they are less than we are. Even when they enter far into our world, they still think they are less than we are. They are different.[19]

But are they really so different or do the middle classes want to believe that they are in order to retain their own sense of being protected from the horror of the lower-class lifestyle? Adams herself concludes that many of the poor actually want to

> swim in the middle of the stream, to live the same lives, maintain the same standards, as their better-paid neighbours. Sadly, many of them found themselves pushed off towards the mudflats of society, unable indefinitely to continue to stay afloat [. . .] If they chose not to make a fuss, to

shut their mouths tightly and just plough on, they usually had their reasons. Reasons born out of lifetimes of experience which told them that rocking the boat could only lead to capsize.[20]

While these books about the poor state clearly that they do not want to incite revolution, they also insist that through their research they wanted to show the dignity of the lives of the poor. They wanted to make visible not only their poverty, but also the way they cope with it and how they continue to express determination, sheer grit and 'almost unbelievable optimism and joie de vivre'.[21] But is not dignified here synonymous with silenced?[22] Do middle-class people really want to hear how the poor live; i.e. do they actually let the poor speak? Ben Cheever openly admits that he is not really talking about the other poor people he encountered on his voyage to their world by saying:

This book's greatest failure is that it's turned out such a personal story. I am the character I talk about most. So it seems as if I'm the only character who matters. Please know that this is not what I think. I am selling Ben Cheever. Not because he's the best product. I'm selling Ben Cheever because he's all I've got. It wouldn't have been fair – or legally advisable – to reveal everybody else's life as if it were my own. Instead I've had to reveal my own life as if it were everybody else's.[23]

In the final analysis, these books about the lives of the poor reflect the move from the ideology 'Be yourself' to the propagation of its failure. The writers thus write primarily about themselves and express their feelings about poverty from the distant point of view of an observer who is only taking a tourist trip to the land of the poor. However, their message is also that work necessarily brings failure to the poor.

Yet these accounts about the lives of the working class do not calm the anxieties of the middle class who have in the last years lost the economic security of their jobs. Anxiety and depression have paralysed many former employees of dot.com businesses. Some speculate that women cope differently than men with the loss of job: 'For most women, survival trumps ego; they simply adapt and find some job. For men, grappling with joblessness inevitably entails surrendering an idea of who they are – or who others thought they were.'[24] We will look closer at gender difference with regard to anxiety in the next chapter but, as regards joblessness, we can see how important for keeping anxiety in check is the identification with the symbolic place that one occupies in the social network.

AGAINST CONTINGENCY

What, therefore, is the logic of this search for the secret of how people really live? At first it looks like today's virtual world demands a quest for some kind of reality and that people are searching for what is behind the imaginary simulacra that dominate our perception of the world. Interestingly, this search for the real actually produces more virtuality. Let us look at the so-called reality shows on TV. One explanation for them might be that people who are tired of the virtual would like to see what real life really looks like and that the TV market has simply been playing on this desire by producing reality shows like *Big Brother*, *Survivor* and so on. However, what is exposed to the public on these shows is not an actual reflection of reality. The people featured in these shows very much *play* their parts. While they do not try to adapt to some prescribed role, they actually play themselves: they create a certain image, a persona that they perceive will be of interest to the public.[25]

What happens when one virtuality is supplemented by another? A paradoxical answer might be that it is precisely this supplementation that gives rise to anxiety. Let us go back to Lacan's famous dictum that 'anxiety is not a signal of a lack, but the absence of the support of lack'. Lacan exemplifies this by pointing out how what provokes anxiety for the child is not the absence of the mother, but rather her being constantly close by. In this context, what is horrifying is not the loss of the object, but the presence of the fact that objects are not lacking: i.e. when the mother has been suffocating the child with her presence, the child has no chance to develop desire; the mother's continuous presence thus incites anxiety precisely because the child experiences no lack.

If we return to the example of 'reality TV', we can say that while the continuing presence of the camera tried to capture the failures, contingency and spontaneity of everyday life, it did nothing but create another spectacle. 'Reality TV' tried to reveal the secret of daily interactions, but actually concealed this secret – one might say that the secret of everyday life is its very boredom, its non-eventfulness, as well as the unpredictability and contingency of the events. While 'reality TV' tried to come close to this secret it did nothing but eradicate it for, instead of boredom, we got the participants' excessive attempts to be interesting and thus engaging in strenuous exercises, self-help talk, a culture of fake tribal customs, etc.

In this supplementing of one virtuality with another (which presents itself as something real) what provokes anxiety is not that the idea of Big Brother (the controlling agency from Orwell's novel) has become materialized, but rather that the lack is lacking – i.e. that there is no place for inconsistency, non-wholeness. Thus, when in our virtual world we search for the secret behind the virtuality by filming reality, we are doing nothing but negating the very inconsistency that pertains to reality – i.e. we are trying to get rid of precisely the lack that marks the social. Contingency might appear as horrifying but, in the end, what really produces anxiety is the attempt to get rid of it.[26]

The way anxiety is presented in the popular media gives the impression that anxiety is the ultimate obstacle to the subject's well-being. Anxiety is perceived as something that prevents the subject achieving full satisfaction in his or her life and that should thus be minimized as much as possible or even totally annihilated. One of the advertisements for the anti-anxiety drug Paxil thus depicts a series of families in which one of the partners is feeling sad, out of sorts, overwhelmed or anxious, which causes the worry and unhappiness of the other partner. However, when the troubled spouse starts taking Paxil, happiness returns to the family and life seems full of promise again. This ad gives the impression that, with the proper drug, family life can be fixed quite easily, but the side-effect of such advertising is also the feeling of guilt if one does not opt for a quick drug-fix. Here again, we have at work the ideology of 'Just do it!', i.e. take the drug and life will be great again, while not taking the drug can also be understood as a rejection of getting oneself and the family in order.

Great too can be success in failure, which we learn from the Coca-Cola advertisement entitled 'Life tastes good!' In the TV clip we see a grandson visiting his grandfather who asks him how his studies are going. The young man responds that he is taking a year off. Then the grandfather enquires about the last girlfriend and the grandson admits that he already has a new one. Grandson then asks how his grandmother is doing, and the grandfather informs him that she has moved in with their friend from the bridge club. At this point both men salute each other with Coca-Cola and we are reminded that life tastes good.

This advertisement very much depicts the reality of today's family life where the stability of relationships is a thing of the past. Things have changed for young and old, but now the advertising depicts what used to be perceived as failure (not studying at school, break-ups of relationships) just as change and continues to remind us that life is good anyhow. Contemporary consumer ideology is constantly persuading us that the subject is just a work of art, that 'being' has given way to 'becoming', and that the new self is just an unfolding story continually being updated and re-edited. Such re-editing one can also observe among corporations which today struggle for continuity and thus want to create an image about themselves that will pass into the future. Similarly, parents also try to do it 'right' so that they will not only create an ideal object – their child – but also be nicely remembered by their offspring. Thus one finds a refusal to deal with contingency in today's child rearing, although we know from psychoanalysis that no matter which guidelines we try to follow we cannot predict what kind of effect our parenting will have on our children, since we can never control the way our unconscious slips out in our planned behaviour. However, in today's advice-ridden society, where we no longer have the old (of course, always conflicting) relationships with authorities, we also do not have the type of advice on how to raise children that grandparents used formerly to pass on to their children. Frank Furedi's book *Paranoid Parenting* makes the lucid observation that today's parents seeking advice no longer get answers on how to deal with a troubled child. When they look into books or on the Web, they usually just get advice on where to get more advice – links to more books, more Web pages, more therapists, etc. The search for advice on how to run one's life, from finding a partner, to dealing with children, grooming the body or surviving at a work-place, can in the final instance be taken as another attempt to find a coherent big Other that might help to keep anxiety in check.

Four

Love relationships always rely on a particular anxiety. For a child the anxiety over the loss of love of the primal caregiver is one of the first traumatic moments, and in later life anxiety seems to form an essential ingredient of any future love relationships. The very feeling of falling in love is coupled with a feeling of anxiety that can sometimes prevent the subject from pursuing his or her love interest. At the moment we fall in love, we have our subjectivity temporarily suspended in another subject, which is why we experience an anxiety which shatters our previous self-perception. But when we have found a partner and established a love relationship, we are then often anxious that we may lose their love.

In today's culture where anxiety is publicly perceived as something that has to be annihilated or at least minimalized, and where some gurus of the self-help industry are convincing people that love is just a matter of choice, one witnesses the emergence of an advice culture that tries to find solutions to the anxiety of love. In this chapter, we will look at how writing love-letters seems to be an activity especially liable to cause anxiety, which is why people have often in the past searched for intermediaries who will compose love-letters on their behalf, and today look to the Internet to alleviate their anxieties about love. One can thus find numerous

Internet sites offering detailed advice on how to address a beloved with the help of a love-letter (or an e-mail). On one site, for example, we find the following instructions:

Clear your desk and your mind of distractions.

Place a picture of the one you love in front of you.

Put on your favorite music.

Take out your best stationery and pen.

On another sheet of paper, make two lists: (a) his/her unique qualities; (b) your hopes for the future together.

Personalize the salutation. 'Dear ——,' or 'To my darling ——,' are both fine.

In the body of the letter, begin by telling him/her what you think makes the individual so special. List at least three qualities, ideally emotional, physical, and spiritual ones.

In the following paragraph, share your hopes and dreams for the future you can have together.

Personalize the closing. 'I will love you always,' 'Loving you forever,' 'My heart is yours,' are all good possibilities.

Don't forget to sign!

Spray the letter with a light fragrance.

Address, seal, and stamp the letter.

Wait a day before you send it; you may change your mind.

Drop it in the mail, and look forward to the response.

On other advice sites, would-be letter writers can also purchase all the necessary equipment (stationery, special stamps, pens, etc.) to complete the task. And there are lots of additional tips on how to write a successful love-letter like 'Don't mention anyone else but yourself and the addressee in the letter', and 'Make sure you only send a love-letter to someone who will appreciate it'. For those who still find writing love-letters a far too complicated or time-consuming task, special

Internet sites offer to compose a love-letter. A lover using this service gives a cyber-Cyrano some basic information about the beloved and Cyrano then composes and sends a love-letter (or even a break-up letter) for the lover.

But the most interesting part about the Internet craze with love-letters is the fact that lots of people send various e-greetings and love-letters, not to some distant lover, but to themselves.[1] (One wonders if they also send break-up letters to themselves.) This information might at first seem surprising, but with love-letters there is always a question who is actually their addressee. The artist Sophie Calle in one of her shows exhibited a love-letter that her former lover wrote to another woman; but Calle decided to cross out the name of that other woman and wrote her own instead. As part of her art project, Calle thus simply wrote a love-letter to herself. This supports Jacques Lacan's claim that a subject who writes love-letters actually does not address the beloved but writes letters to none other than himself. No matter how much a lover tries to capture in the letter the essence of his beloved, he is primarily addressing himself, i.e. he is dealing with his own desires, fantasies, narcissism – all that constitutes his in-love feeling. At the same time, the writer of the love-letter is also in a particular way dealing with anxiety; however, as this chapter will show, this anxiety differently affects men and women.

In literature and in the cinema we find many stories in which someone offers to write love-letters for someone else in order to appease that person's anxieties related to the expression of love. However, the one who puts his writing skills at the service of a friend often himself falls in love with the intended recipient. While it is easy to understand how the act of writing a love-letter can provoke anxiety, it is harder to comprehend why the person who offers his writing services to allay the fears of a friend often falls in love with the addressee of the letter.

Anxiety in love primarily concerns the fact that lovers always love in the beloved what he or she does not have – what Lacanian psychoanalysis calls object small *a* – and also offer to the partner nothing but their own lack. However, in the way people deal with their own lack and the lack in the Other, one can see clear differences between hysterics, obsessionals and perverts. This chapter will analyse these differences by looking at three cases: the 1940s melodrama *Love Letters* (William Dieterle), the famous play *Cyrano de Bergerac* (Edmond Rostand) and the more contemporary film *Law of Desire* (Pedro Almodovar).

LOVE LETTERS: HYSTERICAL DESIRE

Questions about the desire of the Other provoke the most anxiety, since the subject on the one hand questions who he or she is for the Other, but on the other hand is also perturbed by what the Other really wants. In love relationships, these dilemmas especially haunt hysterics who often try to find solutions by forming love triangles. The film *Love Letters* presents an illustration of the hysteric's love anxieties, especially their problems with desire of the Other. This film also shows how there is no need for the subject to actually encounter the other person in order to fall in love, but need only create a fantasy scenario around the sublime object that he or she perceives to be in possession of the Other.

In *Love Letters* the protagonists create love fantasies in a complicated triangle between the soldier Allen who writes love-letters for his friend, Roger, which the latter sends to his girlfriend Victoria. Through the process of writing letters and reading Victoria's responses, Allen falls deeply in love with Victoria. After the war, when Allen learns that Roger has died, he decides to find Victoria. By chance, Allen comes across a beautiful woman called Singleton who has lost all her memory of the past and who is supposedly holding a terrible secret. Allen discovers that Singleton is actually Victoria and that she has been accused of murdering Roger. Victoria has been deeply unhappy since her husband did not resemble the character she felt in love with from reading the love-letters. One evening, when Victoria was again reading the old love-letters, Roger angrily threw the letters into the fire and told Victoria that he was not their author. In the next scene, we see Roger lying dead on the floor and Victoria in total shock next to him. Although charged with Roger's murder, Victoria has lost all memory of the past. (Later, however, we learn that the true murderer was a loving old aunt who tried to free Victoria from her husband.) At the end of the film, Victoria recovers her memory and realizes that she has been all the time in love with Allen, since he was the actual author of the love-letters.

It is not uncommon for a subject to form a desire for the object of another's affections. Allen develops an interest in Victoria first of all because of Roger's attraction to her, and Roger finds Victoria even more interesting when he becomes the intermediary of love-letters in which he clearly observes Allen's desire. The collaboration between Allen and Roger thus helps both of them to stay in love with this mysterious woman whom Allen once calls a 'pin-up girl of the spirit'.

Here we have a case of hysteria, since a hysteric is constantly concerned with questions about desire. The subject thus first gets attracted to what he thinks is the object of the desire of the Other, then guesses what kind of an object he is for the Other but, since he can never get a satisfying answer to the question about the desire of the Other, the subject interprets and finds an answer in a fantasy that he creates.

Both Allen and Victoria fall in love with the help of a fantasy which they form around object *a*. While Roger is at first a kind of postman who helps Allen and Victoria keep their fantasies alive, later, when he marries Victoria, he starts to function as an intrusive intermediary who shatters them. It is significant that Victoria developed amnesia when she learned that the love-letters she received were a fraud and that she had not been such an object of desire for her husband as she believed. At this point, Victoria's fantasy collapsed and amnesia helped her not to face the truth about her own and her husband's desire. After Roger is killed, Victoria becomes a 'different' woman: where Victoria appeared like an innocent girl, Singleton looks like a mysterious beauty who holds a sublime secret, and when Allen falls in love with Singleton, he is attracted precisely by this secret. Thus, even before Allen learns that that Singleton is actually Victoria, he is fascinated by something in Singleton that is greater than herself – another name for this secret is, of course, object *a*.

Returning to the problem of hysteria, it could be said that the greatest hysteric in this story is actually Victoria. Both Allen and Roger fall in love with Victoria because they are fascinated by the desire of the Other, but Victoria is the one who constantly questions what kind of an object she is in the desire of the Other. Her conflict with Roger is precipitated by the fact that she does not recognize herself in his desire as she has recognized herself in the love-letters, and it is crucial that she suffers amnesia only until she realizes that Allen is the true author of the letters. In this context we can read Victoria's loss of memory as some kind of hysteric symptom in which she finds a temporary solution for the traumas related to her love life.

CYRANO DE BERGERAC: OBSESSIONAL DESIRE

In the case of the hysteric, love-letters are often a means of dealing with his or her questioning of the desire of the Other, and from such letters a hysteric can thus get some relief to the anxiety-provoking question as to who he or she is for the Other. However, in the case of obsessional neurosis, love-letters can be an attempt to prevent a horrifying encounter with the desire of the Other. An example of this strategy can be found in the famous play *Cyrano de Bergerac*, whose main character, Cyrano, is secretly in love with the beautiful, young Roxane. Believing he is too ugly because of his large nose ever to win Roxane, the eloquent Cyrano helps Christian, a tongue-tied soldier, to woo her with love-letters. After many years, Cyrano tries to tell Roxane the truth, but Christian is killed in battle and Cyrano feels compelled to keep his secret. Years later Roxane, living in a convent and still faithful to her husband Christian, is visited by her mortally wounded friend Cyrano. It is then that she realizes that Cyrano was the beloved author of the love-letters. His secret revealed, Cyrano dies as he had lived, heroically and fearlessly.

Cyrano is a typical example of an obsessional neurotic for whom the object of desire is too overwhelming and thus who actually tries to keep this object at bay, in this instance by writing love-letters for someone else. The obsessional is afraid that by coming too close to the object of his desire, the object will devour him and make him vanish and, in order to protect himself from this anxiety-producing object, he creates all kinds of rules, prohibitions and obstacles, which become the cornerstone of his love life. When at the end of the play these obstacles vanish and Cyrano comes too close to Roxane, he tragically dies. It appears that once there was no barrier between Cyrano and his lover, he could not continue being in love and live happily ever after, and that writing love-letters for someone else and thus preventing an actual encounter with the object of his desire was the necessary prerequisite for keeping Cyrano's love alive.

Cyrano is an especially interesting figure because we have here a particular problem with the phallus. The whole play is centred around the fact that Cyrano has a huge nose which appears as some kind of a phallic obstacle in his love life. When Cyrano admits to his friend that he is in love with Roxane, he himself points out that he cannot expect that his love will ever be realized because his nose makes him unattractive. However, when Cyrano has a verbal exchange with some bore who seems to make mockery out of him, he makes a big fuss out of protecting the grandeur of his nose. When Cyrano asks: 'tell me why you stare so at my nose?' he gets no answer from the bore, but then Cyrano goes on and on with questions like: 'What is there strange? . . . Is't soft and dangling, like a trunk? . . . Is it crook'd, like an owl's beak?. . . Do you see a wart upon the tip? . . . Or a fly, that takes the air there? What is there to stare at? . . . What do you see?' The bore does not answer to these questions, and only remarks: 'But I was careful not to look – knew better.' To which Cyrano responds: 'And why not look at it, an if you please? . . . Oh! it disgusts you! . . . Its hue Unwholesome seems to you? . . . Or its shape? . . . perchance you think it large?' The bore staggeringly responds: 'No, small, quite small – minute!' Then Cyrano becomes even angrier:

> Minute! What now?
> Accuse me of a thing ridiculous!
> Small – my nose? . . .
> Tis enormous!

Old Flathead, empty-headed meddler, know
That I am proud possessing such appendice.
'Tis well known, a big nose is indicative
Of a soul affable, and kind, and courteous,
Liberal, brave, just like myself, and such
As you can never dare to dream yourself,
Rascal contemptible! For that witless face
That my hand soon will come to cuff – is all
As empty . . .
Of pride, of aspiration,
Of feeling, poetry – of godlike spark
Of all that appertains to my big nose.[2]

So, although Cyrano is supposed to be impeded because of his nose, he at the same time takes it as an organ which gives him enormous power. And here, the nose does not seem to be an obstacle, but rather an asset. It looks as if having such a large nose that it distorted his face, Cyrano developed his language skills to compensate. He was thus able to acquire a symbolic power instead of counting on the power of a beautiful body. In this context, it is as if Cyrano replaces a phallus-like physical organ (which is an obstacle) with a symbolic phallus – his language skills. However, it is crucial that, in his attempt to seduce Roxane, Cyrano needs an intermediary – Christian.

When Christian first meets him he makes fun out of Cyrano's nose, but Cyrano overlooks this offence since he knows that Roxane is attracted to Christian. Christian feels extremely happy on hearing this news, but then Cyrano ruins his enthusiasm by saying that Roxane expects a love-letter from him. Christian then says: 'I have a certain military wit, / But, before women, can but hold my tongue. / Their eyes!

On Anxiety

True, when I pass, their eyes are kind ...' Cyrano then guesses: 'And, when you stay, their hearts, methinks, are kinder?' But Christian responds: 'No! for I am one of those men – tongue-tied, I know it – who can never tell their love.' To which Cyrano confesses: 'And I, meseems, had Nature been more kind, / More careful, when she fashioned me, – had been / One of those men who well could speak their love!' Christian feels sorry that he has no eloquence, but Cyrano offers him a deal: 'That [eloquence] I lend, If you lend me your victor-charms; / Blended, we make a hero of romance!'[3] Hence, true to say only two men together then can make an ideal love partner for a woman?

Lacan in his unpublished seminar on anxiety points out that a man takes a woman as a vase in which there is supposed to be a hidden object, while he also behaves as if there is hidden in the vase the phallus of another man. This can be illustrated, for example, by the case of a man who falls in love with a woman who has previously been the lover of someone the man admires, or that of a woman who has a father that a man identifies with. Lacan points out that the object *a* fills the vase after the subject has undergone castration. But it is essential that the object comes from somewhere else – it is constructed only via desire of the Other. If Allen in *Love Letters* falls in love first of all because the woman (Victoria) is Roger's girlfriend, in *Cyrano de Bergerac* it is crucial that Cyrano incites Christian to pursue Roxane, but then does all the work for him. Thus, Allen and Cyrano both function as some kind of father figure – or even phallic figure – who secure the love relationships that are formed between the person they desire and another man.

The fact that love anxieties have to do with subjects falling in love with what is in the Other more than him- or herself, becomes all the more complicated when we introduce the problem of sexual difference. The major problem of the male and the female subject is that they do not relate to what their partner sees in them.[4] Lacan in his formulas of sexuation pointed out that both men and women are attracted precisely by what the Other actually does not possess: however, while a man searches for a sublime object in a woman, she searches for a symbolic power in a man.

Psychoanalysis links symbolic power to phallus, but the phallus one finds on the male side is nothing man can be happy about, for, although woman relates precisely to this phallus, man is not at all in control of it. Man thus constantly tries to take on his symbolic function, since he knows that the symbolic function is what the woman sees in him. However, he necessarily fails in this attempt, which causes his anxiety and inhibition. As Lacan points out: 'The fact that the phallus is not found where it is expected, where it is required, namely on the plane of genital mediation, is what explains that anxiety is the truth of sexuality . . . The phallus, where it is expected as sexual, never appears except as lack, and this is its link with anxiety.'[5] For men, the way they desire (which is crucial also for the relation they form with the object *a* on the side of their partner) is conditioned by the fact that castration marked them by a lack – which also means that their phallic function has been negated. As a result of this negation, men are anxious that they might not be able to do it: that their organ might deceive them at the time they will need it most, that others might find them powerless, etc. Lacan points out that it is because of this anxiety that man created the myth of Eve being made out of Adam's rib, which allows him to think that if just a rib was taken out of him then he is essentially not missing anything, i.e. there is no lost object and therefore the woman is just an object made of the man. Although this myth tries to assure men of their wholeness, it nonetheless fails to alleviate their anxiety, which often emerges precisely when a man encounters a woman who becomes an object of his desire.

For Lacan it is crucial that a man gives up as lost the hope of finding in his partner his own lack, i.e. his fundamental castration. If this happens everything works out well for a man: he enters into the Oedipal comedy, thinking that it is Daddy who took the phallus from him, i.e. that he is castrated because of the law. This comedy helps a man in his relation-ships; otherwise, the man takes all guilt onto himself and thinks that he is 'the sinner beyond all measure'.[6]

What about a woman's problem with castration? A woman is also a split subject and is thus concerned with finding the object she does not have; she is also caught in the mechanism of desire. However, for Lacan the fundamental dissatisfac-tion that is involved in the structure of desire in the case of women is pre-castrational: a woman 'knows that in the Oedipus complex what is involved is not to be stronger, more desirable than mother, but to have the object'.[7] Thus the object a is for a woman constituted in her relationship with the mother. Lacan also claims that a woman only becomes interested in castration $(-\varphi)$ in so far as she enters men's problems, which means that castration is a secondary thing for a woman. As a result: 'For a woman it is initially what she doesn't have as such which is going to become the object of her desire, while at the beginning, for the man it is what he is not, it is where he fails.'[8] A woman is thus concerned that she does not possess the object that a man sees in her, thus she constantly wonders what is in her more than herself; and because of this uncertainty, she endlessly questions the desire of the Other.

In short, a man is traumatized by not being able to assume his symbolic role and a woman by not possessing the object of the Other's desire. This gives us an answer as to why some men are so concerned to keep intact their well-organized life and dread encountering the woman who provokes their desire. Clinging to self-imposed rules gives a man at least temporary assurance that the symbolic order is whole and that it might have endowed him with phallic power. But coming close to the object of desire opens the possibility that this fantasy will collapse and the man will then be stripped naked, exposed in his essential impotence and powerlessness.

Returning to *Cyrano de Bergerac*, we can say that being exposed in this nakedness and impotence is precisely what Cyrano fears. At the beginning of the play, Cyrano explains to a friend that he loves the fairest lady of the world, 'Most Brilliant – most refined – most golden-haired! . . . She is a danger mortal, all unsuspicious – full of charms unconscious, like a sweet perfumed rose – a snare of nature, within whose petals Cupid lurks in ambush!' However, Cyrano then goes on that he cannot get close to this girl ('this danger mortal'), because of his nose. When he sees some knight with a lady on his arm, he fantasizes that he might be able to do the same, but when: 'Thought soars to ecstasy . . . O sudden fall! – The shadow of my profile on the wall!' When his friend encourages him that ladies actually love his wit and that, from the way Roxane with great concern observed his duel, she must love him in her heart, Cyrano answers: 'That she mocks my face? That is the one thing on this earth I fear!' In the context of the above explanation of men's anxieties, Cyrano's fear of having his face mocked or, worse, to be laughed at because of his nose, can easily be explained as an anxiety that his phallic power will be exposed in all its impotence. And at the same time, we can also say that his fear is precisely not to lose his nose, his last protection from the devouring object.

For the obsessional it is crucial that the way he imagines the woman supports him in his phallic position, while at the same time, he has to prevent himself from coming too close to the dangerous *jouissance* that the woman possesses. As Jacques-Alain Miller points out: 'The obsessional subject must ascertain that all *jouissance* be accounted for; all must be signified. This means that all *jouissance* is dead.'[9] Writing love-letters is one way to signify *jouissance*. But Cyrano prevents any encounter with *jouissance* in a double way by writing letters for someone else.

If men often answer to their love troubles by extensively clinging to obsessional rituals and self-imposed rules (which are supposed to prevent them from being overwhelmed by the object of desire), women's dilemma with the question of what kind of an object they are for the man can result in rejection of love and in its place an immersion in melancholic indifference. One often finds gestures of resignation in women who realize that they have not been loved as they had hoped or when they acknowledge that they have ceased to be the object *a* around which a man's love-fantasy used to be formed. In *Love Letters* Victoria finds a temporary solution to her dilemmas in amnesia, which presents a form of retreat from her old world; and in *Cyrano de Bergerac* Roxane's seclusion in the nunnery can also be understood as a kind of resignation, which allows her to cling to her old love fantasies.

It is crucial that in both cases women without knowing it find particular enjoyment in a doubling of their partners. If one of the lovers in both cases looks like a young, beautiful hunk who cannot master his language, the other resembles a father-like figure who is well versed precisely with words.

Does the woman always need a father figure as well as a lover? And are fathers actually writing love-letters for the lovers, in concealment, as it were? If we go back to Lacan's image of the vase in which a phallus has to be hidden so that a man might see in the vase the object *a*, we can speculate that the myth of the *Cyrano* might very well be as much a fantasy for women as it is for men. If men deal with their love anxieties so that they become writers for other men, women deal with their anxieties by always having more men in store, and especially by having some kind of father figure in the picture.

LAW OF DESIRE: THE PERVERT'S TRAP

If *Love Letters* and *Cyrano de Bergerac* both deal with the idea that the subject needs an intermediary in order to fall in love and stay in love, *Law of Desire* takes another turn. Here we have Pablo, a gay filmmaker who is very much in love with Juan, while young Antonio is in love with Pablo. The latter also has a sister, Tina, who changed her sex from male to female. Pablo writes love-letters to Juan, but Juan's responses are noncommittal. Frustrated, Pablo types up a letter to himself and sends it to Juan with instructions to sign it and send it back. When the letter arrives, Pablo is highly satisfied, but when Antonio reads it, he becomes extremely jealous, seeks out Juan and kills him. Devastated, Pablo temporarily loses his memory after a car accident and becomes a suspected killer of Juan, while Antonio falls in love with Tina not knowing that she is actually a man. At the end, when police surround the apartment in which Antonio is hiding, Antonio and Pablo passionately make love one last time, before Antonio shoots himself.

In this complex plot we have many problems stemming from love and desire. However, let us focus on Pablo's love-letters. Pablo knows what kind of an object he wants to be for the other – that is why he simply composes a love-letter he wants to receive from his lover. When the signed letter arrives back, Pablo reads with great joy that Juan cannot wait to see him and is curious about what is going on in Pablo's life. Pablo is not questioning what the Other's desire is or what kind of an object he is for the Other – that is why he does not fall under the category of hysteria or obsessional neurosis. Pablo is certain what brings him enjoyment, which is why clinically he would be much closer to perversion than neurosis. While the neurotic constantly has questions with regard to desire, the pervert has an answer – he has found satisfaction and has no doubt about what he or the Other wants.

If one might find traits of perversion in Pablo's writing love-letters to himself, Antonio's obsession with Pablo reveals a case of psychosis. Antonio's passion for Pablo looks like a passion without intermediaries; i.e. some kind of an immediate relation to the desired object.[10] At the beginning of the film Antonio, after seeing Pablo's movie, which depicts homosexual eroticism, masturbates in the cinema lavatories and repeats the phrase 'Fuck me, fuck me' that was uttered in the film. Very soon, when he meets Pablo and they make love for the first time, Antonio positions himself as the character in the film who demands to be penetrated by his partner.[11] With this sex scene, Antonio looks like repeating the scene he has just seen in the movie; however, it is crucial that, from the time Antonio first saw Pablo's film, the latter becomes an ultimate object of desire for him. There seem to be no boundary that can prevent Antonio possessing this object. When an obstacle emerges in the form of Pablo's former lover Juan, Antonio simply decides to get rid of him by killing him. Paul Julian Smith makes an interesting observation that the Antonio character in the film looks like a 'void', without a past: 'As the figure of passion, absolute and unqualified, he is deprived of the gaps or "fissures" . . . of other characters.'[12] Antonio thus looks like a subject who is not penetrated by a lack and who also has no questions in regard to his desire or desire of the Other.

Although we do not learn anything about Antonio's past, the film exposes the fact that Antonio has an obsessive German mother who is constantly spying on him. Antonio insists that Pablo needs to sign his love-letters to him with a woman's name, because he is afraid of his controlling mother. Since Antonio show obvious signs of psychosis, one can speculate that there has been no separation between mother and child in this case, i.e. no intervention of the symbolic law, which is why Antonio also feels no guilt for the act of murder that he committed. As Chapter Five will show, the psychotic does not feel anxiety with regard to legal prohibitions, and has no doubts that any crime he may have committed was the right thing to do.

What has changed in today's love relationships? The invention of cyberspace and virtual love did not change much of the logic of courtly love that we know from the past. Although today it can happen that the love object to whom a writer addresses his love-letters over the Internet may not even be a human being, but simply a computer that fakes human responses, the mere act of writing can still very effectively incite feelings of love. But more interesting than the phenomena of falling in love with a fictitious person is the fact that lots of people today send love-letters to themselves. One can easily understand that a woman might write herself a valentine card in order to provoke the jealousy of her desired man, one has more difficulty understanding a person who sends themselves an e-greeting which no one else will read. These new kinds of communications that people establish with themselves open up the question of whether something has radically changed in the subject's structure, and especially in his or her relationship with the big Other.

As we have shown, the neurotic constantly questions what kind of an object he is for the Other, while the pervert does not have this dilemma – he has a certainty that he is the object of the Other's *jouissance*. Because of this certainty, the pervert rarely enters into analysis and does not try to get from the Other answers to the questions of who he is, and what he wants. The neurotic who constantly deals with these questions is supposed to come to a point at the end of analysis when he does not hystericize himself in the same way and does not expect from the Other a word about his being. What if the subject seeks to avoid the dilemmas about the desire of the Other by simply writing love-letters to himself?

In the seminar *Encore*,[13] Lacan points out that love always involves some uncertainty. Since the lover loves what the Other does not have, i.e. the lack in the Other, the subject can never get from the Other a desired answer. Lacan goes even further to suggest that knowing what your partner will do is not a sign of love. Love is linked to the fact that in the end we know nothing about the object that attracts us in the Other, and that at the same time the Other knows nothing about this object that is in him more than himself, i.e. what makes someone attracted to him. But today it looks as if we try to alleviate this essential anxiety that comes as part of love. People do not want to deal with uncertainty, so either become more and more enclosed (i.e. are able to maintain mostly only cyber-relationships which allow them to never actually meet the partner) or want a very precise answer from the Other (and are buying tons of self-help books which will supposedly help them to figure out the desire of the Other).

But do we have, in the case of people sending love-letters to themselves, some kind of generalized perversion? As we have shown in our example, *Law of Desire*, a pervert has no doubt about the question of what kind of an object he is for the Other. However, in the case when people over the Internet write love-letters to themselves, we cannot say that we have a case of perversion. Rather, in this case we are dealing with neurotics who still continue to pose questions about the desire of the Other, and since the Other cannot answer, they interpret the desire of the Other and answer in its stead. Today it looks as though the subject who perceives him- or herself as an autonomous rational subject who is always able to make informed choices, cannot easily deal with the fact that the Other is barred by constitutive lack. And, in order not to deal with this inconsistency of the Other, the subject himself constructs the answer who he is for the Other and just 'puts' this answer in to the computer's 'mouth'.

In writing love-letters, one is constantly left with the impression that one does not know how to express love in a proper way or that the words necessarily fail to express the deepness of love. Of course, a similar dilemma also concerns talking about love. In *Love Letters*, Allen says to Singleton (Victoria): 'I couldn't possibly say what I'd like to say right now.' Singleton asks: 'What?' and Allen responds: 'I'd like to say you're lovely.' To which Singleton responds: 'Go ahead, say it. I'd like to hear it.' Together with this problem that one cannot fully express love with words goes the problem that the Other cannot give a proper response. (When we talk about the failure of speech with regard to love, we should also not forget the famous saying of Le Rochefoucault that men love only if they can talk about love. There is no love outside of speech.) But people who constantly search for advice either on how to talk properly about love or try to create answers from the Other are, of course, never going to find the ultimate advice.

Let us finally return to Sophie Calle. One of her most interesting art projects was done in the early 1980s when Calle found on the streets of Paris an address book, which belonged to a man named Paul. Calle decided to learn as much as possible about this person by contacting people whose phone numbers were in this address book. Each day, Calle met with one of these people and for a whole month *Libération* published her reports on these meetings. From people's recollections about Paul, we slowly learned lots of things about his profession in documentary film-making, his love passions, his odd life routines, and even the fact that he was now away at a film seminar in Norway. When Paul returned to Paris he was shocked that he had been the object of such an art project and wrote a furious response to the magazine. Paul took the project as an extreme form of violence – an as utter intrusion into his private life. But he also stated that as a documentary film-maker his idea is that one should never try to get to grips with another person's life by simply looking at the person from the outside, i.e. taking seriously other people's reflections on him or her, but should always give voice to the person in question.

Sophie Calle and Paul never met (at least not at the time of the art project). However, Calle's writings about Paul can almost be understood as special kinds of love-letters – although they were addressed to the general public, in the final instance, they very much addressed Paul himself. Paul is a sublime object of attraction which the letters attempt to decipher and come close to. But these letters failed in this attempt. Paul's disgust with them especially shows how the subject can never respond in a way the writer might have expected.

The relation between Sophie Calle and Paul seems like a failed rapport, however, as we know from psychoanalysis every sexual relationship has failure at its core. Paradoxically, it is from one of Calle's reports on Paul that we can nicely see the logic of such failure in love life. One evening, Calle met with Paul's former lover Claire who passionately recounted a film idea which Paul wanted to realize. Calle writes:

> And then she tells me about one of his ideas, an adaptation of the invisible man: one day the invisible man, exhausted by having to play all the double games, hides in a store case to cry about his solitude. People pass by without seeing him. But one woman stops and comforts him: she is blind. What follows is a love story between the invisible man and the blind woman. They flee in a small boat. You see the oars moaning by themselves and the woman in the front, her face turned toward the horizon. This is the last shot.[14]

One can say that in the relationship between Sophie Calle and Paul, he wanted to be the invisible man (i.e. not be exposed in public) and she was the blind woman who, no matter what she wrote about Paul, did not 'see' his essence. But, nonetheless, let us close by speculating that the affair between an invisible man and a blind woman actually might be an ideal love story. Since the invisible man has his eyes intact, he can admire the woman's beauty and be attracted to what is in her more than herself. While at the same time, this man does not need to obsess with the question of how the woman sees him and the woman does not need to be disappointed by what she sees. Perhaps the best solution for Cyrano is truly to become an invisible computer operator who sends love-letters but is not perturbed by women's gaze.[15]

Five

Today we are witnessing an anxiety related to parenting that stems from the fact that there is no longer any consensus on how best to raise one's children and influence their development. The anxiety that one is not doing a good job as a parent, and the feeling of guilt that one has failed one's children has encouraged numerous authors to form guides to parenting which unfortunately, however, often contradict each other in this advice. This chapter will look at extreme cases of anxious parenting that resulted in infanticide or other forms of child abuse. These examples will help to clarify the difference between anxious parents who constantly have doubts about their actions and thus search for advice on how to do the best job in parenting, and those who lack this doubt, but are still anxious about their children's well-being. The first type of parents usually fall into the category of neurosis and are constantly searching for the big Other that would give them consistency, the latter have an ignorance with regard to the big Other which also makes them much less concerned about social prohibitions. In order to understand how important it is that the subject feels anxious with regard to these prohibitions, let us first look at the most striking case of infanticide that recently happened in the United States.

On 20 June 2001, Andrea Yates, a very religious Texas

mother, waited for her husband to go to work and after break-fast, drowned her five children one by one in a bathtub. She then laid their dead bodies on the bed, wrapping the hands of the boys around the baby Mary, and called the police. To the sergeant she said that she did not hate her children and was not mad at them; she killed them because they were not develop-ing correctly. Yates admitted that she had been considering this act for two years, since she realized that she had not been a good mother to the kids: 'My children weren't righteous. They stumbled because I was evil. The way I was raising them they could never be saved. . . . Better for someone else to tie a millstone around their neck and cast them in the river than stumble. They were going to perish.'[1] She said to the jail doctors that nothing could mute the pattern that said that she was a lousy mother and that the death of her children was her punishment, not theirs: 'It was . . . a mother's final act of mercy.'[2]

Media reports on Yates repeatedly described Andrea as the most devoted mother, who home-schooled her children, orchestrated special family events, took great care of her ailing father, cooked food for the relatives and was also an obedient wife who relied on her husband for decisions. Yates's family was very religious and followed the teachings of the travelling Evangelist preacher, Michel Woroniecki, who held apoca-lyptic views about the end of life of our consumerist society and the dangers of sinful mothers. All five of Yates's children had biblical names and the family expected to have as many children as God would give them. However, after the crime, it became known that Andrea Yates had a history of psychotic breakdowns, which got worse with every additional child and which especially escalated after the delivery of her last child – baby Mary.

The State of Texas supports a very narrow understanding of the defence of insanity, which demands from the prosecutors only that they establish whether the defendant knew the difference between right and wrong. Since Andrea Yates herself called the police after her act, it has been easy for the prosecutors to claim that she knew that her act was legally wrong. Although psychiatrists who acted as expert witnesses for both defence and prosecution testified that this was a severe case of psychosis, the psychiatrist hired by the prosecutors insisted that Andrea Yates nonetheless knew the difference between right and wrong. Andrea Yates was thus found guilty and sentenced to life imprisonment.

Yates's case opens up a very particular type of anxiety that pertains to the mother–child relationship. Early psychoanalytic discussions on anxiety centred on the traumatic relationship that the child has towards his or her parents – at first especially to the mother. In this context, birth is supposed to be the first anxiety-provoking event for the child. Today, however, the debates centre on the traumas that mothers experience at the time of delivery. Psychiatry has thus linked post-traumatic stress disorder to the event of giving birth. For the mother, it is not only the moment of delivery that is traumatic, but the very act of becoming a mother. In today's culture of so called 'paranoid parenting', a mother is especially prone to experience constant anxiety over her new symbolic role and suffers from guilt that she is not doing the 'right' thing in regard to her children's upbringing.

Andrea Yates's crime can help us understand also the subject's anxiety in relation to the law: her confession that killing the children was the right thing to do, will allow us to analyse the difference between a neurotic and a psychotic subject's relationship towards legal prohibitions.

If the law judges the psychotic in terms of his or her understanding of right and wrong, it might be very much surprised to find that a psychotic subject has no doubts about what is right and what is wrong and for example might insist that the crime he or she commits was the right thing to do. While the law relies on the fact that the subject feels guilty in the legal context and is also uncertain with regard to his or her compliance with the law (i.e. constantly guesses what the law might define as right and wrong), a psychotic has a certainty in regard to what is right. The fact that psychotics have no anxiety regarding legal prohibitions places them outside the rule of law. How can psychoanalysis help us understand this ignorance about law, which in the case of psychotics often contributes to their criminal acts?

A 'normal' neurotic subject and a psychotic have very different perceptions of reality. While a neurotic subject structures his world in the form of a fantasy scenario which covers up the lack (the real), in psychosis this 'real' often emerges as a persecutory voice or gaze which starts to haunt the subject and as a result of which the subject's perception of reality becomes radically changed or even shattered. Very often, a psychotic commits a crime in order to get rid of this persecutory voice or gaze and thus tries to change his perception of reality. Sometimes, a psychotic will also perceive another subject as a source of danger, and this can result in the most brutal kind of criminal act.

Let us first focus on why another human being might be perceived as dangerous for the subject. Psychoanalysis invokes the notion of the Other that discerns both another human being and the Other of language, i.e. the social symbolic order. While Freud was concerned with the question why encounters with others, especially one's parents, might be traumatic for the subject, Lacan oriented himself towards the structural causes of possible traumas. The encounter with the Other of language causes a particular type of trauma for the subject which Lacan names 'troumatisme'. The word 'trou' in French contains the notions of gap, lack and hole. The subject in his or her encounter with the Other therefore has a problem precisely with the lack in the Other, i.e. with the fact that the Other is not whole, but is inconsistent.

In this encounter with the Other there are however two types of horror. On the one hand, the subject is horrified by the inconsistency of the Other, which in a special way affects his or her relationship with the law. (The neurotic subject, for example, constantly complains about the powerlessness of authorities, inconsistency of the laws and feels insecure because no one seems to be in charge.) But on the other hand, the subject often has the impression that there is an Other who has stolen enjoyment from him or her, i.e. that somewhere there is a powerful authority, which seems to be without lack and thus capable of enjoyment in a way that leaves others deprived.

The subject in his or her relation to the Other of language loses something. Psychoanalysis has from the beginning considered birth to be a traumatic process in which the subject first encounters this loss, which one can perceive as the loss of shelter in the mother's womb and also as the loss of a crucial part of one's body – the placenta. Early anxiety theory was very much concerned with the question of whether anxiety originates in the physical moment of birth. For Otto Rank,[3] for example, birth presented the first traumatic anxiety-provoking experience for the subject. Freud[4] contradicted this theory, pointing out that at the moment of birth the subject does not yet deal with the problem of loss of the object – this comes only later in the relationship with the mother or other primal caregiver.

Lacan perceives the loss that the subject encounters on entering the world as a structural loss. When the subject is marked by language, he or she becomes marked by a lack and, although this is a purely symbolic loss, the subject often perceives it in terms of a loss of a piece of flesh. Or, as Lacan says, the subject seems to be scarifying a pound of flesh when entering into symbolic order.[5]

As I pointed out earlier, the melancholic subject confuses lack with loss, and finds a particular 'solution' to the problem of the lack that marks the subject by insisting on a melancholic attachment to the lost object. An example of this might be a mother who falls into a deep melancholy after giving birth who is unable to deal with her lack; but in cases of psychosis the subject has not been marked by a lack, which is why the mother's crisis here follows another logic. In psychosis, the subject does not feel anxiety over the loss, but rather over the emergence of some terrible persecuting agency.

While a neurotic often feels anxious either through loss of an object or through the emergence of a disturbing object at the place of the lack, for a psychotic anxiety quickly turns into paranoia – the object becomes a threatening, persecuting object. For Andrea Yates this terrible persecuting agency was Satan. (In order to prove that Satan has possessed her, Yates told the doctors to shave her head so they could see the number 666 – the mark of the Antichrist – on her scalp. She also wanted her hair cropped in the shape of a crown, which has been understood as an attempt to win salvation by Jesus.) Previously, Yates had tried to get rid of Satan by killing herself, but failed in the attempt. Later she decided that the only way to save her children from the fires and torments of hell was to kill them before they reached adolescence.

The particular relationship that a subject has to this terrible object that fuels their anxiety can help us understand how vastly different cases of infanticide can be. While Andrea Yates tried to get rid of Satan and not her children (she very much believed that by killing her children, she provided a better place for them in heaven than on earth), other mothers might kill their children because they present an obstacle to their self-perception.

INFANTICIDE AS A WAY OF DISCOVERING A WOMAN BEHIND A MOTHER

Faced with the crime of infanticide and the horrific forms of violence that a mother can inflict on her own children, the public might well feel as if the shocking story of Medea keeps on repeating itself. The parricide and incest of that other mythical figure, Oedipus, pale in comparison with Medea's crime, especially as Oedipus committed his offences in ignorance, whereas Medea acts out of calculation – she knows that by sacrificing her children, she will hurt Jason the most. Horrified by the knowledge of what he has done, Oedipus makes himself blind, while Medea seems to be without remorse. Even today, the most shocking cases of infanticide are still those in which the mother shows no feelings of guilt after her act.

We see the Medea-type of child sacrifice in the case of Susan Smith, who in 1994 sank her car in a lake with her two boys strapped inside. For ten days Smith played the role of a mother in distress because a black man allegedly kidnapped her children. After she confessed her crime, the horror of her act became especially hard to comprehend, in light of the fact that she tried to rid herself of her children in order to secure the love of her boss's son, as if she wanted to abandon motherhood in order to reclaim some part of femininity that men might find attractive.[6] How can we understand this act?

For Freud motherhood was one of the ways in which women might try to overcome their lack by finally possessing something – a child that would make them complete. Lacan however, insisted that no object can fill the lack that marks the subject, and that motherhood is no solution for women's dilemmas through being a split subject. For some women motherhood might even open up the problem of feeling they have given up on some *jouissance*, so that someone might make an attempt to reclaim the position of the 'true woman' by distancing herself from the position of motherhood. While a mother insists on the position of having, a 'true woman' exposes her lack and is willing to sacrifice her possessions.[7]

Medea is a tragic example of a woman who gives up her dearest possession in order both to wound Jason by taking away what is most dear to him, as well as to be viewed as a woman and not as a mother in the eyes of her man. But as Jacques-Alain Miller points out this attempt of women to insist in the possession of not having, i.e. to embrace their lack and thus appear as true woman, also takes other forms. There seems to be 'no limit to the concessions that a woman can make to a man with her body, her soul, and her possessions. "Concessions" here means to give up. This means that every woman is capable of going as far as not-having and of being a woman through not-having.'[8]

In contrast to women who are able to embrace their lack (i.e. not-having), men are much more burdened by having. Some men are thus constantly afraid that they will lose something and as a result may be more covert than women in their behaviour. As we saw in the last chapter, Cyrano was just such a man, who was afraid of losing status if someone were to mock his nose, which is why he also did not want to come too close to his beloved woman.

Susan Smith seems to be prepared to sacrifice her possession in order to be perceived as a 'true woman'. In contrast to Medea, Susan Smith does not seem to want to hurt her former husband by taking away what is most precious to him; rather, she seems to be primarily concerned to appear seductive for the boyfriend. She seems to be burdened with the image of motherhood to such an extent that she perceives that her new lover might not desire her unless she uncovers some true femininity in herself.[9]

How does Andrea Yates's crime differ from Susan Smith's? Although Andrea Yates did not have such hysteric dilemmas with her femininity as Susan Smith did, her psychotic delirium nonetheless coincides with motherhood. Yates started having severe psychological problems after the birth of her fourth child. At that time, she became more and more withdrawn: 'Staying in bed all day, she scratched four bald spots into her scalp and picked sores in her nose. She used her nails to score marks on her legs and arms in her silent obsessions.'[10] She also experienced visions and voices: 'She would hear commands: "Get a knife! Get a knife!" ' She first saw this image of a knife and a person being stabbed after the birth of her first child, and after the fourth child she again saw this image with the bloody results. Afterwards, she was briefly treated by a psychiatrist, who prescribed injections of anti-psychotic drugs, which Yates perceived as 'truth serum' and hated the way they caused her to lose control of herself. She tried unsuccessfully to commit suicide to get rid of the persecuting voices.[11]

There were two very important attachments in Andrea Yates's life: first, to her ailing father, and second, to the travelling preacher Michel Woroniecki, who often expressed his extreme religious views in private letters to Andrea. In one of them, he wrote 'that "the role of the woman is derived . . . from the sin of Eve" and that bad children come from bad mothers.' And it was after the death of her father that Andrea's situation rapidly worsened: 'She became absorbed in the Bible. . . . She constantly held baby Mary but would not feed her. She stopped talking. She went days without liquids. She began scratching her head to baldness again.'[12] After a brief hospitalization where she received anti-psychotic drugs, the psychiatrist discharged her with optimistic advice: 'Think positive thought.' At the meeting with the psychiatrists, Andrea's husband Rusty did all the talking, and Andrea was simply a quiet woman who showed no signs that she wanted to exit her silence.

A psychoanalyst assessing Yates would have looked at a variety of elements that seem to have contributed to her act. It is significant that her mental condition radically worsened after her father's death. We do not know much about her father other than that he had been suffering from depression and Alzheimer's disease. In addition, one of Yates's brothers is supposed to suffer from bipolar disorder and there are other reported cases of mental illness in the larger family. With regard to Andrea's act, one should also question whether the sex of the last child had a particular meaning for Andrea. From her husband's reports they expected first to have enough boys for a whole basketball team and afterwards a girl might arrive. Did the fact that she gave birth to a girl in any way affect Andrea, since during one talk with a jail psychiatrist, she mentioned that for the prophesy to be fulfilled, it might have been enough to sacrifice only Mary?[13] Why did she regret that she did not sacrifice only her? One would also need to look into the transferential relationship that existed between Andrea and her mentor Michael Woroniecki who has been publicly preaching that 'the whole world is going to hell', that 'multitudes are going to hell'; and that 'God doesn't give a hoot about your little selfish affluent self-oriented world'.[14] In psychoanalysis, it is well known that there might exist so called 'folie à deux' – a form of madness in which one copies the act of another. However, Woroniecki did not himself commit an act that Yates copied, and although it is quite possible that Woroniecki is himself delusional, the difference between him and Yates is that he has been able to 'socialize' his delusions, i.e. make a specific religion out of it.

American women's organizations and women celebrities have taken Yates's case as an opportunity to raise public awareness about the isolation, stress and loneliness of motherhood and thus try to show the underside of the publicly embraced image of the devoted mother whose whole life revolves around children. Thus a clear case of psychosis exposed the pathological undersides of the publicly embraced image of motherhood (as well as revealing the conflicting attitudes that even 'normal' mothers have towards their children).

Some feminists publicly perceived Andrea Yates as a horrible symptom, in which the dark side of conservative ideology suddenly came to surface and where God-fearing fundamentalism coupled with the devoted mother's protective love of her children resulted in the most horrible violence. However, in doing a critique of fundamentalist religious views on women and exposing the stresses of motherhood, one would nonetheless be mistaken in viewing Yates's act as something precipitated by that conservative ideology.

Psychoanalysis is very clear in pointing out that an outside event or ideology cannot be the cause of a subject's fall into psychosis unless the psychotic structure was already in place before, although the subject might not yet have developed a full-blown psychosis.

Why is it that an ideology, like Christian fundamentalism in Andrea Yates's case, cannot push the subject into psychosis? First, we need to note that the psychotic stands outside normal social relationships, which also means outside the law. Since the symbolic law has not been operative in the psychotic upbringing, he or she is not marked by a lack and also not bothered by the fact that the Other is lacking. That is why a psychotic has a relationship outside the law – in contrast to the hysteric who is constantly questioning whether law is consistent and just, a psychotic does not have similar doubts. The psychotic subject is not divided and thus shows no doubt – he or she 'knows'. Although psychotics might seem very religious, they are actually non-believers, because they produce their own answers. In contrast to hysterics who have lots of doubts about what God wants, how they might be judged by God, etc., psychotics have certainty – they know what God's message is. There is a certain innocence in this position of psychotics – the Other is always the one who is in charge and persecutes them, controls their thoughts, etc.

Andrea Yates's explanation of why she killed her children expresses this kind of psychotic certainty. She expresses no doubts about the satanic danger from which she tried to protect her children. She shows no remorse for her act, and even when she acknowledges her guilt, she does it with an expression of innocence – she perceives herself as a bad mother who was trying to get rid of the real danger in the form of the satanic enemy.

The media have been puzzled why Yates called the police and calmly admitted her crime. In light of the psychotic's outside relationship to the law, this gesture presents no surprise. The psychotic might very well know the law, while he or she does not internalize social prohibitions in the same way as the neurotic, who may constantly question what the law allows and what it does not, may feel extremely guilty for the 'crimes' he or she never committed, or may even commit a crime in order to test if the law will be able to find him or her. The psychotic, on the contrary, does not try to figure out whether the law is inconsistent or not, but treats it as an outside mechanism which does not touch his or her inner self.

With regard to a subject's relationship to the law, one can thus discern clear differences in cases of neurosis, perversion and psychosis. While the neurotic, who has been marked by a lack (i.e. castrated), has doubts about the consistency of the law, feels guilty before outside prohibitions as well before the superego, the pervert often tries to take the law into his own hands in order to complete the castration that has not been fully installed. Here, a good example might be a masochist who enjoys making a contract with his mistress and demands to be punished. Often, a pervert will also commit a form of crime and then let himself be caught by the law, as if with this gesture trying to make law operative.[15] A psychotic, on the contrary, does not seek punishment to alleviate guilt as the neurotic might do, or to make law operative, as the pervert might wish. A psychotic will have ignorance in regard to law, which again shows that he acts from the position of supreme innocence and does not fear law's punishing power. He might very well perceive law as an authority which will help him fight other persecutory powers, as Andrea Yates does with regard to satanic influences. Although Yates at some point supposedly said to the jail psychiatrist 'I deserve to be punished. I am guilty',[16] her guilt did not relate to the legal prohibition of killing, but to her guilt in front of God. Yates strongly believed in state-sanctioned exorcism and thus perceived George Bush as a saviour who, by punishing her would save her from the clutches of Satan. Since Scripture teaches that the government is a minister of God, the state's execution would rescue Yates from the evil inside her.

RELIGION AND PSYCHOSIS

The case of Andrea Yates has been particularly troubling for the public to come to terms with since it is hard to comprehend how a loving mother can kill her children. Another disturbing factor in this case is the role played by religion. Most commentators who at the time of the trial predicted that one couldn't expect Yates to be proclaimed insane, backed this up by pointing out that in a very religious country like America, the public would have a hard time perceiving religious feelings as delusions.[17]

In this regard, it is not surprising that the legal debate about Yates's state of mind did not invoke an old critique of the standard M'Naghten test which deals with the question of how the law can decide the way a defendant who suffers from religious visions understands the difference between right and wrong. This question touches on whether religious visions can be taken as proofs of insanity or not. As early as 1915 American lawyers debated how the law should respond if the defendant claims to hear the voice of God telling him or her to kill. In the case of a man who killed a woman claiming that God had told him to do so, Justice Benjamin Cardozo formulated so-called 'deific decree doctrine'. This doctrine criticizes the M'Naghten test by pointing out that it asks only if a person knows the difference between legal right and wrong, not whether they can also distinguish between moral right and wrong. In his reasoning, Cardozo gave the following example:

> A mother kills her infant child to whom she has been devotedly attached. She knows the nature and quality of the act; she knows that the law condemns it; but she is inspired by an insane delusion that God has appeared to her and ordained the sacrifice.

Cardozo's conclusion was that it seems a mockery to say that, within the meaning of the statute, the mother knows that the act is wrong.

Justice Cardozo has an almost saintly status in American legal history, since he has been regarded as the embodiment of virtue and benevolence and has often been compared to St Paul, St Francis of Assisi and Thomas More. His conclusion from the example above was that such a case of infanticide would present the strongest case for finding the defendant insane, and that it would be abhorrent to hold the defendant criminally responsible. So, under Cardozo's understanding, a defendant might very well know that their act is legally wrong, but if because of religious delusions they think that the act was morally right, law should assume them to be insane. This deific decree doctrine, established with the help of Cardozo's loving parent example, has rarely been claimed and when claimed, has rarely been successful. Some take this as proof that apparently 'there are few devoted mothers or affectionate fathers who either hear God's command to sacrifice their children, or who respond obediently if they do'.[18] However, Andrea Yates's case shows that Cardozo's critique of M'Naghten should not be so quickly forgotten.

A mother's relationship with her child often involves a particular fantasy scenario, and it is through this scenario that her desire is mediated. The mother loves her child with the help of this fantasy – she makes a story, a scenario around what is in her child more than him or herself – the object *a* – the object that is a stand-in for the lack that marks the subject. In psychosis this fantasy scenario does not exist: since here the object *a* has not been excluded from the symbolic, no fantasy has been formed to cover up its lack. That is why an object, which is a stand-in for the lack of the Other and is as such inaccessible, in psychosis appears as real. When this object suddenly materializes in the body of the child, the mother might feel she has a direct relationship with it.

How does such destruction of the child relate to love? Lacan's famous saying about love is: 'I love you, but, because inexplicably I love in you something more than you – the *objet petit a* – I mutilate you.'[19] Every love concerns the fantasy structure that the subject creates around this 'something in the other more than him or herself'. But while a neurotic subject will hystericize him or herself with questions about the nature of the sublime thing in the Other, as well as what the Other wants and how the subject appears in the Other's eyes, the psychotic has no such dilemmas. A neurotic mother might constantly ask herself what her children want, whether she is doing the right thing, if she is a good mother, how society perceives her, etc. In contrast, a psychotic mother does not have these doubts – she has certainty. Andrea Yates knows that she is a bad mother and thus needs to protect her children from herself.

What happens to a psychotic's love? Is a psychotic capable

of love? In some way, every act of falling in love has a touch of delusion. The first moments of infatuation are often experienced as a kind of delirium in which the subject aggrandizes the Other and perceives him or her as someone possessing the object *a*. For the neurotic however this delirious state will be coupled with questions like 'How does the other perceive me?' or 'Who am I for him?' – but a psychotic continues to have a special relation precisely with the object *a* in the Other. This object, which in psychosis returns because it has not been excluded from the symbolic, then becomes the psychotic's partner. In the psychotic delirium, the Other in the meaning of the symbolic order or another human being loses its identity and takes on a spectral image of the persecuting voice or gaze. The persecutor is then simply an image or another with whom the only possible relationship is aggression or eroticism, without the mediation of the symbolic. Such eroticism has been at work in the famous case of Judge Schreber, who in his delirium felt that he was becoming a woman who had a special relationship with God.[20]

For the psychotic, the encounter with an enjoying or a desiring Other can be most traumatic and can easily provoke them to commit a crime that may appear to have no obvious motive. However, it is often the case that the psychotic tries to discover him- or herself in the image of the Other, and that there is certain transitivism at work in the violence of the psychotic. In Andrea Yates's case it is obvious that the enjoying Other was the Satan: she perceived herself as possessed by him – or, rather, incorporated him into her own body. Her scratching of her head to reveal the number 666 there clearly shows that she wanted to expose the dangerous Other in her, as well as get rid of it.[21]

A mother's violence towards her children can reflect a number of anxieties. The case of Andrea Yates illustrates the way a psychotic mother might feel anxious because of the emergence of a persecutory object (Satan, for example), while that of Susan Smith shows how the mother's anxiety can turn into violence because of her attempt to keep her lack, i.e. to be perceived as a woman and not as a mother. One can find a very different type of mother's violence and anxiety in cases of 'Munchausen syndrome by proxy' (MSBP). Invoking the famous story of Baron Munchausen who almost drowned but then rescued himself by pulling himself out of the water by his hair, MSBP designates behaviour of someone who induces an illness or a somatic symptom in another in order then to be able to save him or her. This syndrome is primarily used to describe cases of overprotective mothers who insist that their children are ill and then go from one doctor to another in search of cures for them. Often children might even show particular symptoms when in the company of the mother, while when they are alone these symptoms quickly disappear. In such cases it looks as if the mother is overtly anxious about the well-being of her child but, behind the facade of her concern, one often finds the mother displaying a particular brutality and ignorance towards the child when she thinks that her actions are not observed, while in the presence of others she acts as the most devoted and loving parent.

Some theorists of MSBP think that for such mothers the special transferential relationship they develop with the doctors is of crucial importance, since they try to come close to persons of authority. While this search for authority might very well signal that such a mother is a hysteric, more complex cases often show a psychotic structure at work and even some perverse enjoyment. The mother seems to be driven by a particular *jouissance* and does not care for the well-being of herself or the child. Behind her concern for the child is therefore an aggression which feels like something stronger in her than herself – she seems to be pushed by a force that can very well mutilate the corpse of the child or make him or her ill.

An interesting example of MSBP is the case of Elizabeth H., a woman who came from a closely knit, religious family, married at the age of 21, had a daughter Amelie and then divorced her husband. Amelie has been hospitalized ten times in the first two years of her life for failure to thrive and intractable diarrhoea. The mother insisted that the little girl was intolerant to any food, other than mother's milk. The child has been submitted to numerous medical exams, which however showed no illness. After Amelie lost half a pound of blood and started losing her hair and teeth, a dentist suggested that she should be tested for mercury poisoning (however these tests were never performed). At the age of 2 Amelie died and Elizabeth insisted that no autopsy be performed.

Elizabeth at first fell into deep depression, but then quickly had another child, Danny. This child, too, supposedly developed intolerance to any food, other than mother's milk. Until the age of 5, Danny was then fed only mother's milk either directly from her breast or frozen in the form of Popsicles.[22] Danny's childhood was a tortuous experience of continual visits to doctors and endless clinical tests. Although these tests failed to show anything wrong with the child, because of a falsified medical history he was prescribed drugs by various different doctors.[23]

When a local newspaper published a distressing story about the gravely ill Danny, who according to his mother had survived the rigours of his incurable disease longer than anyone had before, doctors, police and social services started to intervene in a new way. Danny was hospitalized, but no illness other than asthma was confirmed, and doctors also realized that Danny had been thriving quite well on his diet of mother's milk only because he had been 'sneaking' a wide variety of foods at home over the years. When Danny's case was discussed in court, the child protection agency insisted that Danny should remain in his mother's care but that they should both undergo psychotherapy, while the doctors hoped that he would be removed from his mother's care. In the end, Danny remained with his mother, but his condition rapidly deteriorated. He was taken to hospital many times because of asthma attacks and there were suspicions that the mother had not administered proper dosages of the medication prescribed for his asthma. These asthmatic traumas finally resulted in a respiratory arrest, causing a permanent neuro-cognitive deficit. On the day of this arrest, Elizabeth dropped Danny off at a park where he came into contact with known asthma-inducing conditions: pollen, grass, dogs and exercise. When he was later in the emergency room, a nurse overheard his mother saying several times 'You can't breathe' and soon after, he suffered a respiratory arrest. The doctors had difficulty inserting a breathing tube because of a tightening of Danny's vocal cords that lined the passageway to the lungs. His mother Elizabeth was completely calm throughout, though Danny's arrest resulted in brain damage and profound memory loss. Afterwards, the court ordered Danny to be assessed by the psychiatrist, who noted that Elizabeth became anxious during any separation from Danny, and that

Danny would adopt a sickly, helpless position, which some-times resulted in self-induced injury.[24]

While anxiety of separation is usually on the side of the child, in the above case we can see that a psychotic mother might also suffer a terrible anxiety. Elizabeth tried to prevent separation from her child by repeatedly fabricating his illness. In this case, mother's milk was perceived as the ultimate object that would forever keep mother and child connected. Mother's anxiety, which at first looks like her concern about the well-being of the child, here results from her inability to separate from the child. Separation of the child from the mother means that mother has to deal with her own lack as well as with the lack in the Other. Mother has to cease using the child as an object that makes her complete, and the child also needs to deal with his or her own lack which a mother's love can never annihilate. A psychotic mother, however, has not been barred by a lack, which is why she cannot separate from the child.

TELLING IT ALL

Beset by a great deal of discussion about trauma and the way to prevent it, parents today often feel that raising children in a way that tries to verbalize all possible traumatic events might prevent a child from forming a trauma. As previous chapters show, one also finds a tendency today to believe that pinpoint-ing potential sources of anxiety can alleviate its effects. These trends go hand in hand with the emergence of the self-help industry, which tries to give guidance on how traumas and anxiety can be mastered. But is it true that a 'telling it all' approach gets the desired result, i.e. prevention of children's traumatic behaviour?

A psychoanalyst, Catherine Mathelin, reports on a case of a

7-year-old boy Arthur who was brought to her by his parents, because he was violent and unruly in school. At the time of the session, Arthur started drawing a picture of a huge sea dragon, a terrible octopus that eats everything up, and a sea elephant that sits on the eggs. Arthur explained that these eggs were all going to die – they were going to be broken and squashed by the sea elephant. Arhur's parents were terribly distressed by these pictures, but their defence was that they had done everything to change their son's obsession. Said the father: 'My wife knows all about psychology. She knows what to do. For example, we never kept any secrets from him; everyone knows secrets are bad.'[25]

The parents explained that they were especially careful to tell Arthur about a traumatic event in which his baby brother suffered brain damage at the time of his birth. After this baby was born, the mother was informed that he would be abnormal, broken, if he survived. Describing this traumatic story, the mother said: 'The brain was broken, that's the word they [the doctors] used, and here's Arthur who draws broken eggs!' The father then interrupted the mother: 'Look, let's not talk any more about all that. You know it makes you ill every time. Arthur knows all about it, and it's got nothing to do with him.'[26] The mother, however, continued the story and recounted how she had told the doctors that if the baby was really broken then they had to 'do something'. The doctors responded that they couldn't comply with such request; in any case, soon afterwards the baby took a turn for the worse and died. After this traumatic event, the mother started guessing whether the baby died a natural death, or whether the doctors stopped the life support, because she had said that she didn't think she was able to take care of a handicapped child.

The psychoanalyst concluded that Arthur's violence, his wish to 'slaughter' everyone, was an echo of his mother's question of whether she was a murderer: 'As if to reassure her, Arthur seemed to be telling her that her secret wasn't so terrible: "I want to kill them, but there's nothing wrong with that." '[27] Although the parents tried to say it all in order to prevent Arthur developing trauma in regard to the death of his baby brother, they could not control their own unconscious, their fantasies or their feelings of guilt. Arthur's drawings reflected his mother's anxiety which was linked to the superego guilt: thus, the sea elephant squashing the eggs does not show Arthur's own aggression, but rather his desperate attempt to appease his mother's anxiety and guilt.

This case puts into another perspective the idea that parents should have no secrets in front of their children in order to prevent possible trauma. With regard to secrets, psychoanalysis relies on the motto: 'To say everything is not to tell all.' No matter how much we try to put into words events, dramas and traumas, we cannot control the unconscious which speaks between the lines of what we intended to utter. Returning to Arthur, it can be said that no matter how much the parents tried to keep no secrets from him, they could not tell all. And it looks as if Arthur used his behaviour to deal precisely with what could not be said – with his mother's unconscious desires and fantasies.[28]

The idea that there should be no secrets and that parents should 'tell all' to their children or that the trauma can be verbalized stems from the illusion that it is actually possible to tell it all.[29] This perception was at work too in the case of Andrea Yates where, on the one hand, we had the perception that Yates should have had a chance to really tell the 'truth' about why she committed her crime, and, on the other hand, we had the desperate attempt to reveal every part of her private life to the public. At the time of her trial, websites were formed on the Internet, not only numerous net-shrines devoted to the dead children with pictures from their daily lives coupled with those from the funeral, but also chapters of the books that were being written about Andrea, testimonies from anyone who ever met her, and, shockingly, one was also able to find all her psychiatric medical records.[30]

If Andrea miraculously were to stop being this silent woman who is constantly spoken for by others (first her husband, and now her psychiatrists), would it be possible to come closer to comprehending her crime? Michel Foucault mentions the case of a man who was tried in court and who pleaded guilty to his crime. To the judge's question: 'Why did you do it?' the man said that he would not explain his motives, but accepted that he would be punished for his crime. At that point the judge lost his nerve and said: 'But the law cannot punish you unless you tell us why you did it.' Foucault draws the conclusion that the law today cannot function any longer, if the subject does not want to express his deep feelings and make a confessional speech about his inner conflicts and motives.

In light of this search for confession, can law judge a psychotic? Courts often proclaim a psychotic as a sane person in order to satisfy the public demand for punishment, and a psychotic might actually find particular satisfaction in this result. Andrea Yates might very well get just another proof from her sentence that Satan truly exists within her and that the state might exorcise it. While such punishment might not be troubling for a psychotic, it is much more problematic for the law. The latter will need to accept that the subject has a totally external relationship to it and is in no way hystericized by the law's definition of right and wrong.

The conflicting relationship that mothers have towards their children is something that public opinion has a hard time grasping. Even Freud speculated that a mother's love for her children might be the type of love in which one does not find the usual mixture of love and hate that one does in other love relationships. But psychoanalysts after Freud have changed this view and started stressing the ambivalent nature of a mother's love.[31] However, this ambivalence is not something one needs to be horrified by: problems for children usually emerge if they are either pure objects of a mother's love or objects of her hate, while a mother's ambivalent attitude paradoxically opens space for children to distance themselves from the mother and thus acquire certain 'freedom'.

Six

In recent years, popular psychology has conceptualized the subject essentially as victim of various traumatic experiences, but lately this conceptualization has moved towards the idea of the subject as survivor. For the subject to make the transition from victim to survivor it is crucial that he or she can make a testimony about his or her suffering. Post September 11 this has become more apparent: not only were we bombarded by a proliferation of accounts of this event, we also got a burgeoning industry 'to help' the people who were most traumatized by it; therapists started competing as to who could offer the more effective treatment – hardly surprising perhaps in a business-oriented, quick-fix society like America. Family members of the deceased were offered various types of grief counselling, of which the most widespread technique is known as de-briefing. This term has been primarily used in the past by the secret services like the CIA, for example, whose officers perform de-briefing on captured terrorists. This is supposed to immediately uncover the secret of the terrorist's motives; the idea is that the terrorist will be caught off guard and thus reveal something he actually would have preferred not to tell. De-briefing strategies used for the people traumatized by the terrorist attacks have been slightly different: here, the idea is not so much to capture the 'secret' – that might lie behind the current depression or other form of despair – but to offer a quick solution, and temporarily calm the victim of a traumatic memory.

A subject who has been traumatized by an event is often anxious lest it is repeated. More than a year after September 11, American media daily reported on people's distress using titles like 'Anxiety rides the A train', 'My survival kit', or 'Don't Worry, Be Ready: Chicken Soup for the Anxious Soul'.[1] These reports show that people tried to appease their anxiety in a variety of ways: 'One Brooklyn woman caught herself wondering if she should keep a wet washcloth in her purse, in case of a nerve gas attack during her subway commute.'[2] Some started preparing themselves by buying duct tape and bottled water, and others by taking courses in first aid, biological and chemical hazards. While 'purveyors of preparedness' were selling it as chicken soup – 'Whatever's ailing you, it can't hurt' – many people were searching for an antidote to anxiety, though some recognized that all the security measures actually had the opposite effect – they made people more anxious.

Psychoanalysis has from its beginning recognized a link between anxiety and trauma. While trauma pertains to the situation of helplessness, anxiety often occurs as a signal that reminds a subject of a possible repetition of the traumatic situation. An anxious subject thinks: 'The present situation reminds me of one of the traumatic experiences I have had before. Therefore I will anticipate the trauma and behave as though it had already come, while there is yet time to turn it aside.'[3] Freud concludes that anxiety is on the one hand an expectation of a trauma and on the other a repetition of it in a mitigated form. As Chapter Two showed, anxiety is an anticipation of helplessness that is associated with a danger situation, but to the known *real* danger the subject attaches an unknown *instinctual* one:[4] if real danger seems to threaten a subject from an external object, neurotic danger threatens him or her from an instinctual demand. However, as Freud points out, in so far as the instinctual demand is something real, the subject's neurotic anxiety can also be admitted to have a realistic basis.[5]

Therefore anxiety can be perceived as a signal which tries to protect the subject from a trauma. However, in some situations this is reversed, so that traumatic memory offers a particular solution for the anxiety state. As pointed out in Chapter Three, in today's society anxiety is linked to the fact that, on the one hand, no one seems to be in charge and, on the other, that someone might be in charge in a hidden way (which opens the door to all kinds of conspiracy theories). These anxieties relating to authority are especially linked to the changed role of the father in today's culture. Freud's theory teaches that anxiety is primarily linked to castration and that in the Oedipal phase the subject has a particular anxiety-ridden relationship with the father. But, as this chapter will show, in some cases of anxiety, traumatic memory can offer a quilting point that helps the subject to find answers to his or her distress with anxiety.

I will look at two cases of how a subject deals with the anxiety related to the impotence of authorities, which in a controversial way relates to the horror of the Holocaust. First, I will analyse how anxiety and trauma are dealt with in Binjamin Wilkomirski's *Fragments* and then in Roberto Benigni's *Life is Beautiful*. Both works present a child's perspective on the Holocaust. The main difference between them is that *Fragments* claims to be an authentic memoir of a 3- or 4-year-old child's experience of a concentration camp, while *Life is Beautiful* has no pretension to truthfulness, but presents the Holocaust in the form of a comedy. These two versions of the Holocaust trauma both reflect on the inner struggles of a child in the midst of horror, and especially on the impact that authorities might have on how an anxiety-evoking event is inscribed into the child's traumatic memory.

FATHER DON'T YOU HEAR ME?

Fragments unveils the memory 'shards' of a childhood spent in the Nazi death camps of Poland. The author, now a musician living in Switzerland, believes himself to have been born around 1939, in Riga, Latvia. When he was 3 or 4 years old, his family was uprooted from their home and after a period of flight during which he witnessed his father's execution, Binjamin was separated from his brothers and his mother and transported to Majdanek, the first of several camps in which he spent the next four years.

Wilkomirski narrates his memoir from the perspective of a confused, frightened child, in disjointed flashbacks, which vividly picture the life in the camps: the hardship imposed on inmates, the cruelty of the guards, the sickening realities of existence, the fear and guilt. There are powerful accounts in the book of bloodied rats crawling from bodies in the camps, of a woman, possibly his mother, giving him her last scrap of hardened bread, of babies who chewed their fingers to the bone before dying, and of his standing barefoot, ankle-deep in excrement in order to keep warm. Binjamin does not know why he survived. The only explanation that he can provide involves the kindness of an older boy named Jankl[6] who slept with him on his mattress and who taught him survival techniques.

The book moves back and forth between the years in the death camps and the years in Switzerland, making no distinction between the two experiences. Initially the victim of Nazi torture, after the war Binjamin became the victim of well-intentioned adults who tried to convince him that he did not experience the Holocaust. His foster parents, for example, insisted that he abandon the strategies of self-protection, which he had acquired in the Nazi camps and, although Binjamin had been able to survive the horrors of the camps, he later felt completely powerless to cope with the banality of good intentions which he was forced to endure in freedom. He thus concludes: 'Friendly grown-ups are the most dangerous. They're best at fooling you.'[7] Although, people were trying to convince him that the concentration camp had been just a dream, he believed that the camp was still hidden somewhere and that guards simply disguised themselves as harmless people, but could kill at any time.

Wilkomirski reflects in many passages of the book on the difficulty of coming to terms with the horrific events that traumatized him throughout his life. At the beginning of the book, for example, he points out how language has been failing him, since he has 'no mother tongue, nor a father tongue either'.[8] And at the end of the book, he explains that he simply needed to write his story:

> I wanted to know everything. I wanted to absorb every detail and understand every connection. I hoped I would find answers for the pictures that came from my broken childhood some nights to stop me going to sleep or to give me terrifying nightmares. I wanted to know what other people had gone through back then. I wanted to compare it with my earliest memories that I carried around inside me. I wanted to subject them to intelligent reason, and arrange them in a pattern that made sense. But the longer I spent at it, the more I learned

and absorbed empirically, the more elusive the answer – in
the sense of what actually happened – became.[9]

Fragments became an international bestseller and its author
got numerous awards but, after all this success, it became
clear that the book was a fraud. Swiss writer, Daniel
Ganzfried, a son of a Holocaust survivor, was the first to claim
that Wilkomirski was not born in Latvia, as his book says, but
in Switzerland in 1941. The child of an unmarried Protestant
woman, he was adopted by a Swiss couple who named him
Bruno Doessekker. Ganzfried has found a birth certificate and
other documents that indicate Doessekker spent the war years
in Switzerland and started school in 1947, a year before
Wilkomirski says he arrived in the country. To help substanti-
ate his Jewish identity, Wilkomirski told Ganzfried he was
circumcised, but Wilkomirski's ex-wife and an old girlfriend
deny this. After this revelation many other Holocaust scholars
have proclaimed the book a work of fiction; yet, even after
this scandal, Wilkomirski insisted that he was telling the truth,
comparing himself to Anne Frank, whose diary was also for a
long time suspected to be a fake.

This highly disputed memoir is the product of so-called
recovered memory therapy. The author himself admits that
he was able to discover his 'origins' only with the help of
a therapist and through detailed research on the victims of
the Holocaust. It is well known that recovered memory therapy is a highly suggestive technique: the therapist does not
listen to the patient's free associations, but tries to lead the
patient to remember some temporarily forgotten trauma,
which usually concerns an abuse suggested by the therapist
himself as the possible cause of the patient's problems. When
a patient suddenly 'remembers' that he or she has been a

victim of violence in the past, one of the main problems becomes how to convince the others about the reality of his or her recovered memory and to get some recompense for the past traumas. In cases of recovered memory of childhood sexual abuse, for example, the patient primarily wants his or her parents or other authority figures to recognize their guilt, to accept the accusations the patient is making and to show remorse for their 'crimes'.

Patients of recovered memory therapy usually have great problems with authority: on the one hand, they complain either about the violence of the existing authorities in their childhood or their passivity in protecting them from violence; on the other hand, they are quick to accept the therapist as the ultimate authority who is able to make the most 'violent' theories about the cause of their traumas.

These problems with authority found in recovered memory therapy need to be analysed in the context of the broader changes in today's society. Consider that recovered memory therapy emerged precisely at a time of numerous dilemmas concerning the status of authority in contemporary society. The last decade has been marked by the decline of the power of traditional authority figures such as fathers, state presidents, church leaders, etc., and the emergence of cult-leaders, sexual abusers, etc. – figures which appear as the obscene underside of traditional authorities. As has often been noted in psychoanalytic theory, the father as the symbolic bearer of the law became in the popular imaginary replaced by the father of the primal horde, a man who has access to *jouissance*, which is for other men inaccessible.

In his second theory of anxiety Freud showed that a son's relationship with his father is a prime source of anxiety and, in his analysis of Little Hans's phobia of horses Freud pointed out that a phobic object often helps to cover up another, more horrible anxiety, which is linked to the particular relationship that the son has with his father. But, although the father can very well be an anxiety-provoking figure for the son, the absence of the father or his powerlessness does not alleviate anxiety. On the contrary, it opens up a space for strong identification with some 'proper' father substitutes (like cult-leaders), as well as a desire to expose the failed actual father. The emergence of recovered memory therapy relates to this demise of authority in today's family which has radicalized the subject's anxieties. But the paradox of recovered memory therapy is that in its war against abusive authorities (like parents and teachers), the therapists themselves often take on the role of leader, and find immense enjoyment in stimulating the stories of abuse.

It is clear from Fragments that its author is deeply troubled by his father's authority. One of the most dramatic points in the book is the description of young Binjamin watching his father being killed by the militia. Wilkomirski writes: 'suddenly his face clenches, he turns away, he lifts his head high and opens his mouth wide as if he's going to scream out. . . . No sound comes out of his mouth, but a big stream of something black shoots out of his neck as the transport squashes him with a big crack against the house.'[10] It is striking that Wilkomirski, who in actuality never knew his father, develops such a vivid memory of the father's execution. It is as if the father failed to utter a word, i.e. to represent the symbolic law – from his mouth comes a silent scream and a stream of blood instead of the voice of the authority. One can even speculate that it is because of this failure of the father to act in the symbolic realm that in his son's memory he becomes a squashed object. This trauma deriving from authorities failing in their symbolic status continues in Wilkomirski's memoir – the real thrust of the book is thus the disbelief in the adults and fear from their 'compassion'. In exposing these traumas, he has achieved enormous identification on the part of his readers. When Elena Lappin tried to figure out why Wilkomirski fabricated his story, she realized that Wilkomirski had been highly convincing in his reports: 'Whenever he talked about the camps, I believed him. His anguish was so genuine. It was impossible that someone could fabricate such suffering simply to justify the claim of a book.'[11]

Jonathan Kozel in his enthusiastic review points out that *Fragments* 'poses questions asked by those who work with spiritually tormented children everywhere: How is a child's faith in human decency destroyed? Once destroyed, how can it be rebuilt? Or can it never be? What strategies do children learn in order to resist obliteration in the face of adult-generated evil?'[12] Kozel even compares *Fragments* to Elie Weisel's Holocaust memoir *Night*, in which

> a fellow inmate confides to Weisel that he has 'more faith in Hitler' than in anybody else. Hitler, he says, is 'the only one who's kept his promises . . . to the Jewish people.' While Wilkomirski never tells us he had 'faith' in any of the brutal 'uniforms' of Majdanek, it is clear that he had more faith in the predictability of their behaviour, once he understood it, than he ever felt in the allegedly kind people who believed they were befriending him in Switzerland. Indeed, for a long time, it appears, he had no faith that what was called 'the normal world' outside the concentration camps was even real.[13]

Wilkomirski thus doubts the reality of the outside world and has great mistrust of the people, while he never doubts the reality of his memory. The only concession he is able to make to the dilemma about the truthfulness of an experience is: 'Legally accredited truth is one thing – the truth of a life another.'[14]

However, the most perturbing question arising from Wilkomirski's memoir is: Why would anyone invent a story that he was a Holocaust survivor? We can answer this question only by looking at the broader discourse about testimony and trauma that dominates today's society. In recent years the growing obsession with memory and trauma has created an idea that one needs constantly to make oneself heard, while there is at the same time no one who can hear one's revelations. It can even be speculated that it is precisely the inexistence of any agency for hearing such utterances that sparked the growth of the testimony-industry as well as recovered memory therapy. Wilkomirski himself says in the Afterword of his book that he primarily tried to find someone who would hear him:

> I wrote these fragments of memory to explore both myself and my earliest childhood; it may also have been an attempt to set myself free. And I wrote them in hope that perhaps other people in the same situation would find the necessary strength to cry out their own traumatic memories so that they too could learn that there really are people today who will take them seriously, and who want to listen and to understand. They should know they are not alone.[15]

Lacanian psychoanalysis has widely discussed the changes in the perception of the big Other that have happened in contemporary society. Today, it is as if we are hoping to patch up the Other by constantly inventing new authorities (like, for example, various committees) that are supposed to provide answers to the insecurities that we face in society. As is well known from Lacan, the big Other as a coherent symbolic order does not exist; however, it nonetheless functions, in that the subject's belief in it has a significant impact on their lives.[16]

One finds in today's society the emergence of a new individualism. The subject is more and more perceived as creator of his or her identity and less and less identifies with the values of his family, community or state. Linked to this ideology of the subject's self-creation is the perception that there is in the subject a truth, which only needs to be rediscovered for the subject to become him- or herself. But if some childhood experience shattered the core of the subjects' identity, they will be deprived in the pursuit of authenticity. Thus we come to the problem of recovered memory: in order to reinstall their equilibrium, subjects have to remember the trauma that undermined their identity. The purpose of therapy in this case is first to discover the original trauma and then to re-create the situation in which it occurred so that the subject's suffering can be alleviated. Examples of such therapeutic approaches are often seen on various TV talk shows. Oprah Winfrey once hosted the famous John Gray (author of *Men are from Mars, Women are from Venus*). Gray asked a young woman to close her eyes and remember which scene from her childhood was especially traumatic for her. The woman remembered that in her childhood her father often told her that she was stupid and now she continuously suffers from low self-esteem. Gray then asked the woman to return in her mind to the original childhood scene and imagine that her now dead father is standing next to her. With her eyes closed, the woman tells her 'father' that he is wrong in calling her stupid, that she actually does not believe what he is saying and that she knows she is intelligent. After a moment of crying, cath-arsis happens – the woman opens her eyes, Gray hugs her as a good father would and from now on her trauma is gone. With the help of the therapist, the woman was able not only to return to her past, but also to recreate this past so that the core of her trauma is gone. Here we thus have a belief that the subject's trauma can be exactly pinpointed to a particular event and, with the help of the subject's imagination, the trauma can be annihilated. In this example it is once again the father who has failed in his symbolic function and with the help of the new father – the therapist – the damage done by the actual father is retroactively annihilated. Equally crucial is the fact that the actual father did not 'hear' his daughter and did not understand his mistakes. However, the woman then finds in the therapist the ultimate believer – the person who not only takes her complaints seriously, but is with his ther-apy able to fix the past, thus appearing as a new God-like creature – a compassionate almighty fixer.

It is well known that Freud insisted that there is no direct correlation between trauma and event. Many subjects can experience an event, but only some will develop a trauma linked to it; while it is also possible that the 'event' never actually happens, but the trauma is nonetheless formed. Analysing the link between trauma and an event, Freud also points out that most traumatic for the subject is not the fact that an event actually happened, but that the subject did not anticipate it and was unprepared. Freud takes the example of a train crash, about which a survivor might only later develop a trauma and become, for example, constantly haunted by the accident in his dreams. By creating an anxiety, these dreams try to make up for the lack of preparedness at the time of the accident, since for Freud it is precisely the preparedness inspired by anxiety that presents the last shield from the shock, and it is when this preparedness is lacking that the event results in a trauma. Which is why Freud says that: 'An individual will have made an important advance in his capacity for self-preservation if he can foresee and expect a traumatic situation of this kind which entails helplessness, instead of simply waiting for it to happen.'[17]

When Lacan deals with the issue of trauma in *Seminar I*, he points out that:

Trauma, in so far as it has a repressing action, intervenes after the fact (*après coup, nachtraglich*). At this specific moment, something of the subject becomes detached from the symbolic world that he is engaged in integrating. From then on, it will no longer be something belonging to the subject. The subject will no longer speak of it, will no longer integrate it. Nevertheless, it will remain there, somewhere, spoken, if one can put it this way, by something the subject does not control.[18]

Here, of course, we have a different idea of trauma from that illustrated by recovered memory therapy. In the case of the latter, trauma is something that needs to be discovered with the help of the therapist and then possibly annihilated via a confrontation with the abuser or a reconstruction of the original situation that caused the trauma; but for Lacan trauma is the hard kernel that has not been integrated into the symbolic: that is why the subject cannot speak about it or refers to it as something external to him or her.

In studies of the Holocaust, it has been often noted that the survivors have great difficulties reporting on their experience from the concentration camps. They often feel as if they have two identities: one related to their present lives, and another from their past traumatic experience; however much they try to put their lives in order, they cannot get rid of this split. The survivors thus often report that they somehow live 'beside' their experience of the Holocaust. One survivor says, for example: 'I have a feeling . . . that the "self" who was in the camp isn't me, isn't the person who is here.'[19]

While Wilkomirski knows that memory from early childhood must look like fragments in which events from various times and places are mixed up, he nonetheless has no doubt in the authenticity of his memory. However, he neither suffers from split identity nor displays any feelings of alienation from the traumatic 'self' from the past, as other Holocaust survivors often do. But a still greater difference between Wilkomirski and Holocaust survivors is to be found in their relations with those who are supposed to listen to their testimonies.

Dori Laub points out that the survivors fail to be authentic witnesses to themselves, i.e. they fail in recounting their stories, because the Holocaust was an event that actually produced no witnesses, because the

> very circumstance of being inside the event . . . made unthinkable the very notion that the witness could exist, that is, someone who could step outside of the coercively totalitarian and dehumanizing frame of reference in which the event was taking place, and provide an independent frame of reference through which the event could be observed.[20]

Laub further explains this lack of the witness by pointing out that:

> one has to conceive of the world of Holocaust as a world in which the very imagination of the *Other* was no longer

possible. There was no longer an other to which one can say
'Thou' in the hope of being heard, of being recognized as a
subject, of being answered. The historical reality of the
Holocaust became, thus, a reality which extinguished
philosophically the very possibility of address, the possibility
of appealing, or of turning to, another. But when one cannot
turn to 'you' one cannot say 'thou' even to oneself. The
Holocaust created in this way a world in which one *could not
bear witness to oneself.*[21]

Holocaust survivors often have great problems in recounting their stories precisely because the perception of the big
Other as the coherent symbolic space in which their address
can be inscribed collapsed in the Holocaust. Thus even today,
the survivors feel the lack of the Other who can bear witness
to their testimonies. But for Wilkomirski the problem is not
the collapse of the big Other – his main problem is how to
get even with individual others (various grown-ups who
represented authority figures in his life).

With this obsession to counter the authority figures who
betrayed him in his youth, Wilkomirski appears much more
like a typical representative of our culture of complaint[22] than
as a Holocaust survivor for whom the very point of making a
complaint has collapsed in the camps, since complaining pre-
supposes the existence of an Other who can answer, while in
the Holocaust even the supposition ceased to exist.[23]

As previous chapters show, Freudian psychoanalysis
regards anxiety as one of the possible ways the subject may
deal with traumatic memory. Anxiety gives the traumatized
subject a certain distance, which allows him to experience an
event differently the second time, for example in dreams and
nightmares. In Wilkomirski's case, however, it seems that a

traumatic memory was produced as an answer to his particular anxiety with regard to the failed father. Wilkomirski's horror of authority figures later becomes just another way of dealing with his trauma regarding his non-existent father. The success of Wilkomirski's memoir is linked not only to the fact that he touched one of the most painful issues of our times – the Holocaust – but also that he addressed the fears that we have about possible abuse by authority figures.[24]

In Wilkomirski's case well-intentioned adults who tried to convince him that his memory of childhood trauma was false turned into the most dangerous persecutors and the non-existence of a father turned into a 'memory' of his violent death. Paradoxically, at the same time that Wilkomirski's book became an international bestseller, we witnessed a strong public identification with an alternative story of a father's authority and the Holocaust. I have in mind here Benigni's much-celebrated film *Life is Beautiful*, in which the father's authority radically intervenes and tries to change the son's perception of trauma. While *Fragments* puts the reader in the position of a helpless parent who tries to find meaning in the fragmented memory of an abused child yet at the same time is powerless to rescue that child from the violence that he has to endure, *Life is Beautiful* offers a triumphant identification with a father who is able to protect his son from the same trauma. This father is however not searching for the meaning of the violence, but instead turns the horror into comedy.

SON'S LIBERATION THROUGH FATHER'S SACRIFICE

Life is Beautiful is a Chaplinesque fable about the power of imagination set against the stark reality of Second World War Europe. At the centre of the fable is Guido, an enchanting individual with childlike innocence and grand dreams of owning his own bookshop. Guido falls in love with Dora, a beautiful schoolteacher, and a fairy-tale romance ensues with a number of comic episodes. When Guido and Dora are happily married and have a little boy, the war starts and the family is deported to a concentration camp. In order to ease his son's experience of the life in the camp, Guido convinces the boy that they have just entered a game, which requires of them many deprivations. If they play the game well and accumulate the largest amount of points, they will be able to win the highest prize – a real tank. The boy very much identifies with the idea of the game; in the expectation of winning the tank, he is able to endure the horrors and deprivations of camp life. Before the end of the war the father dies, but the boy actually wins the game as, when the allies liberate the camp, an American soldier invites the boy to drive with him in his tank. The prize is thus finally obtained.

Here we have the opposite logic to that of *Fragments* or of other Holocaust memoirs. The main problem here is not how to convince the father or other forms of authority about one's suffering, but how a father can persuade his son that the suffering imposed on him is just part of a game. With the idea of the game, the father tries to create a fantasy scenario, which will allow his son to survive the experience of the camp.

It is crucial that the father in *Life is Beautiful* does not play an authority figure that demands direct obedience from his son. He does not ask his son to believe him on his words, when he presents the idea of the game. When the son expresses doubt about the game and says that other children have warned him that that they are all going to be turned into soap and buttons or burned in an oven, the father first reacts with surprise: 'You fell for that? Buttons and soap out of people. That will be the day.' But then, the father agrees that they should just leave the place and allow other children to get the prize, so that what finally convinces the son to stay is the desire of the Other. It is only when the father gives the son the choice and when he trails the idea that others might take their leading place in the game that the son develops the desire to stay. One might even say that the true power of the father does not reside simply in the fact that he created a fantasy game to help his son survive; his ultimate success lies in the fact that he is able to persuade his son to identify with the desire of the Other. The father's true authority resides precisely in his ability to mask his own desire as the desire of the Other.

However, this over-protecting father is too good a figure of authority, and the father's death at the end of the film appears as a necessary sacrifice. If the father has first created the fantasy to help his son survive, by his death the father actually gives his son freedom to detach himself. In the final sequence of the film, the son is thus not only freed from the aggressors, but also from his good father. While there was throughout the film a special bond precisely between the father and the son, at the end, the son reunites with his mother. But the father's legacy is still alive after his death, and when his prediction that they will win the tank comes true, the son gets the final confirmation of the father's authority.

If in Wilkomirski's *Fragments* we have a total lack of 'good' authority figures, which results in the son's utter distrust in the big Other and a desperate search for hidden truth, in *Life is Beautiful*, we have a belief in the father which is conditioned by the belief in the big Other. Thus the fantasy created by the father in the final instance prevents his son from having his belief in the symbolic order shattered.

Some claimed that the success of this fantasy of a father's protectiveness is linked to the guilt of a generation of post-war children who grew up knowing they had been unable to save their own fathers.[25] However, we should not forget that Benini's figure of the protective father looks superficially like a prototype of the impotent permissive father of post-war times. This is the father who seems more playful than the son, who looks shabby, non-authoritarian. However, one can nonetheless conclude that Life is Beautiful brings to surface today's fantasy of an ideal father. He is a benevolent comic representative of the law; a hero who still values sacrifice and is, in contrast to our current fathers, willing to die for his good deed. On top of his sacrifice, this father is also willing to lie to his son, if he believes that this is for the son's own good. This father thus takes on a responsibility, which is otherwise becoming absent in our culture.

When the father in Life is Beautiful dies, he becomes an empty place – an authority in the proper sense of the word (non-existent, but powerful at the same time). The father figure in Wilkomirski's case, however, does not become an empty place – rather, his power becomes overwhelming as he becomes a threatening persecuting agency that gives no space to the son.

It might be hard to imagine that a person would invent a traumatic memory and present himself as Holocaust survivor, while numerous proofs dispute this claim. Nonetheless, one needs to point out that a person with this kind of recovered memory finds in his story special *jouissance*. The fact that recovered memory therapy exposes the obscene underside of authority is usually perceived as a revelation of hidden truth which brings liberation to the subject. However, it is precisely the subject him- or herself who finds special *jouissance* in this search for the *jouissance* of the authorities. Recovered memory therapy takes *jouissance* as the liberating truth, which can serve as the ground for morality; but the result of this endeavour is nothing but the promotion of violence.

The subject fantasizes about the *jouissance* of the Other, because he or she actually tries to supplement the deficiency in the functioning of the big Other. Similarly, the subject often assumes a burden of guilt in order to keep the Other as a consistent order, often claiming responsibility for a crime he or she never committed so that the impotence of the authorities (for example, father, leader, etc.) will not be exposed. One can thus also read the soldiers' guilt for the bayonet killings they never performed (see Chapter Two) as such an attempt to maintain their perception of the consistency of the big Other.

What about Wilkomirski's problem with the big Other? The final enigma of his book is the following: usually, we generate fantasies as a kind of shield to protect us either from unbearable trauma or from anxiety; here, however, the very ultimate traumatic experience, that of the Holocaust, is fantasized as a shield. But a shield from what? Perhaps an unexpected comparison with *The X Files* can be of some help here. As was pointed out by Darian Leader,[26] the fact that, in *X Files, so many things happen 'out there'* (where the truth dwells: aliens threatening us) is strictly correlative to the fact that *nothing (no sex) happens 'down here'* (between the two heroes, Gillian Anderson and David Duchovny). The suspended paternal law (which would render possible sex between the two heroes) 'returns in the real', in the guise of the multitude of 'undead' spectral apparitions which intervene in our ordinary lives. And the same goes for Wilkomirski: for him too the failure of the paternal function results in the fantasy of the most violent horrible event – the Holocaust.

So, we can conclude that the subject invents a traumatic memory because of the necessary inconsistency of the symbolic order and, especially, because of the inherent powerlessness of the authorities. While the case of the soldiers who invented the bayonet killing analysed in Chapter Two demonstrates that subjects often take guilt upon themselves in order to prevent this anxiety-provoking impotence of being exposed, the example of Wilkomirski and other recovered memory cases show that the current dissolution of authority structures have resulted in the idea of the subject as a victim. Here, the attempt is no longer to cover up the impotence of authority figures, but to further expose it. But, as a result of such endeavours, we are often left with nothing but violence and obscenity, which emerges in the form of new authority figures like cult-leaders – as well as some recovered memory therapists.

The cinema seems to be of primal importance in dealing with horrible authorities, but not simply because movies depict a traumatic event in a fictional form. Today, we use passages from the movies to tell ourselves a story of our lives. After Wilkomirski's book became exposed as a fake, it become known that the book not only borrows from the disputed Jerzy Kozinski's novel, The Painted Bird, but also from various movies on the Holocaust, especially the documentary Shoah.[27] Just a few days after September 11, one was able to find on the streets of Beijing films, with titles like The World's Greatest Catastrophe, Pearl Harbor II, and so on, which used excerpts from films like Independence Day, Armageddon, or Wall Street and the like, and mixed them up with the documentary footage from the CNN reports on the fall of the twin towers. Such a response to the trauma of September 11 is very similar to Wilkomirski's dealing with the Holocaust: both take an actual traumatic event and by incorporating it into a fiction create a particular scenario that is supposed to act as an antidote to anxiety. While Wilkomirski tried to come to terms with his own anxiety over authority figures, the Chinese 'film makers' hoped to figure out an answer to the new insecurities that came with the Al Quaeda attack.

Seven

Continual talk about this 'new' age of anxiety suggests to us that anxiety is something that one should get rid of or at least try to control. The way anxiety is presented in the popular media gives the impression that anxiety is the ultimate obstacle to the subject's well-being, and one could easily assume that anxiety is a condition that seriously prevents the subject from functioning in the world and especially from engaging in relationships with others. Thus in recent years, the media has especially focused on so-called social anxiety that the subject experiences in the public domain. Manufacturers of the anti-anxiety drug Paxil, for example, have launched a big media campaign centred on the idea that social anxiety is what prevents people from succeeding in their work and in their personal lives. The first TV and newspaper ads for Paxil showed two images of a man sitting at the table surrounded by people. In the first image, the man is in a straitjacket, while above him is an interrogation light and the people around him have grim, threatening faces; but the second image shows this same scene in a different light – the people here seem friendly, there is no interrogation light, and the man is just calmly sitting at the table. Over the first image, one reads 'This is how it seems', and over the second 'This is how it is'. The text above the images explains how many people today suffer from social anxiety disorder, which prevents them from succeeding in life and at work. However by administering an anti-anxiety drug such as Paxil, it is easy to overcome this disorder. (In small print, of course, are listed numerous side-effects of the drug; however, one gets the impression that even if some side-effects occur, they are well worth the risk, since social anxiety is a far worse impediment.) The message of this advertising is that anxiety radically alters the subject's perception of reality, and that under its influence the subject creates a fantasy, which turns the reality into something dangerous.

Following the terrorist attacks of September 11 advertisers stopped playing on the idea that a person under the influence of anxiety may radically distort reality and perceive it as more threatening than it actually is.[1] The makers of Paxil thus launched a new television advertisement made by documentary film-maker Barbara Koppel, in which real people who were users of Paxil, talk about their struggle with 'generalized anxiety disorder' and how the drug helped them. Instead of suggesting that a subject who suffers from anxiety has a distorted sense of reality, this campaign affirms that the perception of a grim and depressing reality is actually accurate. This gloomy picture, however, is altered to a cheerful and happy one with the help of Paxil. Hence the message of this advertising campaign is that the problem is not that the subject constructs a reality that is not true (since our reality actually is as depressing, hard, and scary as our worst fears told us), but that with the help of Paxil one can experience this harsh reality with new eyes – the grim black and white picture suddenly gets colour, the annoying buzz from the streets turns into soothing music and the subject who has been distressed suddenly becomes a calm and relaxed person. It is also interesting to note how 'generalized anxiety disorder' has replaced the previous 'social anxiety'.

This advertising for anti-anxiety drugs can give us a clue as to what has changed in perceptions of anxiety in today's culture. During the course of this book, I have focused upon two causal factors in this change. First, I have looked at the role of the media in their portrayal of the dangers of terrorism. The discourse of terrorism is constructed in a way that depicts the terrorist as a virus, with regular references to the idea that he may strike anyone, at any time and in any place. The uncontrollable and spontaneous nature of possible terrorist attacks leaves no one feeling safe (an uncomfortable idea for the Western world). Second, I have spoken of the overwhelming anxiety felt by the subject both in private life and in society. Here what has really changed is the subject's relationship with the big Other. This is apparent also from the popular media discussions on anxiety. A self-help adviser on Lifetime television has, for example, stressed five anxieties that hold people back from living their life to the full:[2]

1 There isn't enough (money, love, etc.).
2 They won't like me anymore (i.e. fear of rejection).
3 It is too good to last.
4 I will be found out (i.e. others will see that I am just faking it).
5 My life doesn't matter (i.e. how can I create a legacy for myself).

Advice which seeks to treat such anxieties encourages people to be more generous and less centred on their own wealth; to reveal their real selves, even their flaws; to tack 'I deserve happiness' above a desk or mirror; to create a folder of Positive Enforcements with all the compliments they received so that they can use them when feeling down; to enrich bonds with friends and families, since these relationships are the legacy that one leaves to the world, etc.

Both the list of anxieties and the advice given to overcome them show that the subjects' prime concern is with their place in the world and their interaction with others. Basing the following on Lacanian psychoanalytic theory, I suggest that we can say that most anxiety-provoking for the subject is still the relationship between the subject and the big Other (meaning both other people and the social symbolic network). The Other is for the subject always 'anxiogen'[3], since it constantly forces the subject to ask 'Who am I?', and especially, 'Who am I for the Other?' However, as this book has shown, in post-industrial societies, the subject is also perceived as a self-inventor and as someone who is actually freer from the constraints of other people than our predecessors. So if, on the one hand the subject is still concerned about the question about the desire of the Other (i.e. how others regard them and how they are regarded in society as a whole), on the other hand, the subject is under pressure to make a choice about his or her life independently of social constraints. Thus psychoanalysts often treat patients who come to analysis with the demand 'I need to reinvent myself'.[4] No longer is it the case that they are struggling with parents who prevent them doing something in life, now they struggle with the burden of making themselves into a persona that they might find likeable. As the case of Wilkomirski has shown, this re-making of oneself can sometimes mean change of the most dramatic proportions.

Wilkomirski attempted to overcome strong feelings of anxiety (which were linked to the feeling that he did not know who he was) by writing a book; by finding a 'new signifier',

Wilkomirski hoped he could then make a new self out of the pieces of his own memory. Such an exercise is a way of imaginatively reconstructing oneself. The urge for an anxious subject to construct a new image for themselves is a common way of creating an identity that will be more acceptable to themselves and to others around them.

Lacan distinguishes between ego-ideal, which is on the side of the symbolic and ideal ego, which is on the side of the imaginary.[5] The subject often identifies with some ego-ideal (i.e. authority or ideals that are respected in his or her culture) in order to acquire a symbolic identity, which will inscribe them in a desirable way into society. The identification with the ego-ideal is always a primary one, occurring before the imaginary identification with some ideal ego (i.e. with some image in which the subject appears likeable to themselves). This image (as when subjects observe themselves in a mirror) is always supported by the symbolic, since language and culture determine our perception of ourselves. Whilst it is inaccurate to suggest that subjects live in an imaginary domain where the symbolic does not operate, we can nonetheless conclude that the symbolic today (for example, the media) very much encourages the subject's imaginary identification, so that the subject might well become overwhelmed about the creation of a perfect image.

What kind of anxiety has emerged in relation to the subject's self-perception and his place in society? As previous chapters have shown, anxiety has a particular relationship with desire. Although it is true that we are constantly anxious about the kind of an object that we are in the desire of the Other as well as uncertain about our own desire, paradoxically, our desire, as formulated in fantasy, also offers a protection from anxiety. Fantasy through which we structure our perception of ourselves and the world around offers a scenario in which desire becomes mediated. Thus it is with the help of fantasy that the subject establishes a particular relationship towards the object of desire. Of course, desire is always linked to dissatisfaction, but this dissatisfaction also presents some kind of driving force for the subject. What has changed in today's society is that subjects seems to be less and less caught up in this dialectic of desire and more and more under the pressure of *jouissance*. The popular media bombard people with the demand to enjoy, and offer advice as to how one can find an excess of *jouissance*. One only needs to look at any cover of *Cosmopolitan* magazine to see how the imperative is to have a bigger, better, more ecstatic orgasm, body, career, sense of motherhood, relationship, etc. The pressure for the excess of *jouissance* is coupled with the idea of choice, as well as with the lack of social prohibitions with regard to what kind of *jouissance* is socially acceptable. Paradoxically, this very liberal situation opens up the choice of not making a choice: in the most expensive restaurants today the chef often decides for the guest or, like London's famous chef, Gordon Ramsey, offers the most prestigious meal in the midst of the working kitchen; similarly, expensive television sets remember which programmes viewers like to watch; again, on some motorways, the advertising panels offer specifically tailored ads according to what kind of radio programme one listens to. All these are designed to ease the 'burden' of choice.

On another level, anxiety over too much choice opens up opportunities for new types of gurus and other leaders with whom those who seem most lost in today's society can strongly identify. It is no coincidence that at the beginning of a new millennium, as well as talk about this so called 'new' age of anxiety one also finds strong identifications with leaders who seem to offer answers to our anxieties as well as a clear image of our enemies. Such identifications offer protection from anxiety. If, on the one hand, it looks as if people are keen to protect their individuality, on the other hand, they are also searching for someone to take charge, who will actually take away the very possibility of choice. In a time of an abundance of choice and the imperative to enjoy, it looks as though the subject is actually searching for a master who will regulate his or her *jouissance*. However, this demand for regulation of *jouissance* can easily turn into the horror that the master is actually stealing *jouissance* for himself – i.e. that he is enjoying on the other's behalf.

Psychoanalysis has in recent decades tried to figure out what has changed for the subject at times when the big Other seems to be more and more fragmented, and when the subject seems to be increasingly under pressure from consumerism and constantly complaining about his or her well-being. While the emergence of the so-called 'culture of complaint' seems to be regarded as a negative turn in today's culture, one should rather take it as a sign that the subject still holds a strong belief in the power of the big Other. The fact that the subject remains anxious about whether the big Other exists, or what the Other wants are signs that there has been no turn to a psychotization of society at large. And the very fact that the subject experiences anxiety should not be taken as something that prevents the subject's well-being, but rather as a sign that the subject is struggling in a particular way with the lack that marks the individual and the antagonisms that mark the social. When on the level of society anxiety emerges after times of violence and radical social changes, this becomes a signal that we are faced with the impossibility of signifying these changes. But such a signal also allows us to take more precaution over future progress. In the *Dialectic of Enlightenment*,[6] Adorno and Horkheimer warned that the Enlightenment has always aimed at liberating men from fear and at establishing their sovereignty: but the fully enlightened world radiates disaster triumphant. And at the same time, instead of finding solutions to fear, the Enlightenment actually radicalized it. When an American army commander was asked how he deals with the anxieties his soldiers face before a battle, his response was: 'I am really cautious when I see a soldier who has no anxiety: When I see that special glimpse in the eyes of a soldier which shows that he has no fear of killing, I become horrified.' Society without anxiety would similarly be a dangerous place to live in.

Notes

ONE INTRODUCTION

1 After September 11, news media are daily using the term anxiety to describe how people are coping with uncertainties. A typical report starts like this: 'Anxiety among travelers over SARS and the fighting in Iraq – as well as the transformation of airports into paramilitary zones and disease control centers – heralds an apocalyptic time for the airline industry. The four horsemen are arriving one by one. First came death on Sept. 11, now war and pestilence. What's next?' *The New York Times*, 6 April 2003.

2 Paul Valery, 'The Crisis of the Mind', London, *The Athenaeum*, 11 April and 2 May 1919.

3 The article is significantly entitled, 'Feeling Powerless In a World Of Greater Choice: Consumers Grown More Anxious As They Are Cut Loose in Electricity's New Free Market', *The New York Times*, 26 Sept. 2000.

4 Rollo May, *The Meaning of Anxiety* (New York: Ronald Press, 1950).

5 Thomas Wolfe, *You Can't Go Home Again* (New York: Harper and Brothers, 1940).

6 Robet Jay Lifton, *The Life of the Self: Towards a New Psychology* (New York: Simon and Shuster, 1976), p. 141.

7 For a comprehensive study of conspiracy theories see, Peter Knight, *Conspiracy Culture: From Kennedy to the X Files* (London: Routledge, 2001).

8 This simultaneous danger coming from the outside and the inside has in a particular way been reflected in the struggles that in the last decade shattered the former Yugoslavia. The first paranoia about alleged Albanian separatists (who were under Milosevic's regime renamed into

terrorists) centred on the stories of Albanians trying to poison food in the army. Later, Milosevic's great ideological victory has been that he has been able to create enormous support for his nationalist politics by continuously inventing new enemies and was able to keep alive the fear that there is some ultimate threat against the Serbs. The perception that violence is like a virus which unexpectedly attacks a community has also been the theme of the film *Before the Rain* (Milce Manchevski, 1994), which depicts the nationalist tensions between Albanians and Macedonians. Here the idea of violence as the virus ultimately covers up the political dimensions of the conflict.

9 *The New York Times*, 7 March 2002.

10 Milosevic started to play at The Hague an anti-American hero who at the same time condemns NATO's military actions in the Third World and presents himself as the politician who has only been fighting terrorism all along. Milosevic's 'success' has been that under the guise of constantly finding new possible enemies and thus keeping anxiety alive, he has been able to introduce radical economic and political changes in society without the majority of people paying attention to them. (A propos of these changes, it has been most ironic that after Milosevic's fall, Serbian politicians wanted only to charge Milosevic for his financial manipulations and not for his involvement in the war crimes.) Bush's government, under the guise of fighting terrorists and bacteria, is also introducing radical economic and political changes that seem to go unnoticed by the public. When people feel uncertain and afraid they are in search of clear images of their enemies and they hope that the elimination of these enemies will alleviate their anxiety.

11 *The New York Times*, 17 April 2003.

12 Ibid.

TWO   ANXIETY AT TIMES OF WAR

1 *The New York Times*, 12 April 2003.

2 At the time of the start of the war in Iraq, American media have also reported the overwhelming anxiety of children and their parents' dilemma how to appease them. One mother reflected, 'I am more afraid now than after 9/11', while her little girl was concerned if when the bombs fell on their apartment they should all hide under the bed. *The New York Times*, 13 April 2003.

3 See Sigmund Freud, 'On the grounds for detaching a particular syndrome from neurasthenia under the description "anxiety neurosis" ', *The Standard Edition of the Complete Psychological Works of Sigmund Freud* (henceforth SE), vol. 3 (London: The Hogarth Press, 1962).

4 Ibid., p. 59.

5 Phobia is a particular way to keep this anxiety in check. Often, the subject forms a phobic symptom so that by trying to avoid the phobic object the subject might escape the feeling of anxiety. The best example here is Little Hans. When the little boy develops phobia of horses this becomes for him an attempt to keep his anxiety in check. However, for Freud it is crucial to find out what kind of danger is truly anxiety-provoking for the boy, since it is this danger that the phobic object tries to prevent. Freud finds the answer in the ambivalent relationship of the boy with his father. The real danger for Little Hans is the threat of castration coming from the father. Little Hans feels anxiety in regard to this threat: since he cannot beat this anxiety-provoking threat in reality, Little Hans tries to beat it in the imaginary. He represses whatever incited anxiety and creates a phobic symptom.

6 Freud, 'Inhibitions, symptoms and anxiety', in *The Penguin Freud Library* (London: Penguin Books, 1993), p. 306.

7 For Melanie Klein the first cause of anxiety arises from the inner working of the death instinct. Klein links the primary anxiety to the fear of annihilation. The struggle between life and death instincts starts already at birth. Later the child projects his destructive impulses onto the breast. The child, however, divides the breast into a good and a bad one. The bad one becomes a devouring object the subject is horrified of, but at the same time, the good breast is internalized as the early superego. The child becomes afraid of being annihilated, since 'The frustrating (bad) external breast becomes, owing to projection, the external representative of the death instinct; through introjection it reinforces the primary internal danger situation; this leads to an increased urge on the part of the ego to deflect (project) internal dangers (primarily the activity of the death instinct) into the external world. There is therefore a constant fluctuation between the death instinct acting within and deflected outwards.' (Melanie Klein, 'The theory of anxiety and guilt', in *Writings of Melanie Klein 1946–1963*.) For Klein it is also crucial that this externalization of the internal danger

situations becomes for the ego one of the methods of defence against anxiety.

8 Joan Riviere, 'The unconscious phantasy of an inner world reflected in examples from Literature', in Melanie Klein, Paula Heineman and R. E. Money-Kyrle (eds), *New Directions in Psycho-Analysis: The Signification of Infant Conflict in the Patterns of Adult Behaviour* (London: Tavistock, 1955).

9 Ernest Jones opposed the view that we are most afraid of death by invoking Freud's view that we cannot fear what we cannot conceive of. Since it is impossible for us to have a positive idea of something so negative as being nothing, we can in the final instance be afraid only of the experience of dying, but not of death itself. See Ernest Jones, *Essays in Applied Psycho-Analysis*, vol. 1 (London: Hogarth Press, 1951).

10 Zahava Solomon, *Combat Stress Reaction: The Enduring Toll of War* (New York: Plenum Press, 1993), p. 77. Solomon also reports on cases of psychic numbing when the soldiers felt as if they were already dead and thus stopped feeling anxious. One soldier thus said: 'I wasn't afraid of anything anymore. Because I was dead, and a dead man can't be killed.' Ibid., p. 78.

11 Ibid., p. 78.

12 Lawrence Ingraham and Frederick Manning, 'American Military Psychiatry', in Richard A. Gabriel (ed.), *Military Psychiatry: A Comparative Perspective* (New York: Greenwood Press, 1986), p. 44.

13 Experts also claim that 'a volunteer army is quite likely to be more psychologically resilient than a conscripted one. Trauma endured willingly and in a context of meaning and purpose may yield fewer casualties.' *The New York Times*, 25 March 2003.

14 Ibid., p. 54.

15 *The Wall Street Journal* has reported on the type of ideological propaganda used in the Iraq war where military leaders were convincing the soldiers with the following statements: 'The country will not be at peace, the world will not be at peace, until we eradicate the threat of a new world enemy: international terrorism . . . This is going to be the biggest statement to the world that you are never going to [expletive] with America like that again.' . . . "Take care of yourself, take care of your brother. Don't leave your honour in Iraq. Do what's right. Do what millions of American soldiers have done before you. Do the right thing . . . What we do in life echoes in eternity. God be with you" . . . "I don't

want you to worry about why we're here," said Capt. Anthony Buther, commander of the battalion's headquarters company. "It doesn't matter. When we go north, we are the good guys. We are the cavalry." ' *The Wall Street Journal*, March 20, 2003.

16 *USA Today*, 18 March 2003.

17 See Robert Ursano *et al.*, 'Prisoners of War', in Robert J. Ursano, MD, and Ann E. Norwood, MD (eds), *Emotional Aftermath of the Persian Gulf War: Veterans, Families, Communities and Nations* (Washington, DC: American Psychiatric Press, 1996), pp. 443–76.

18 Michael P. Pinner, Roger J. Peutzien and John M. Mateczun, 'Stress and coping with the trauma of war in the Persian Gulf: the hospital ship USNS Comfort', in Robert J. Ursano, Brian G. McCaughey and Carol S. Fullerton (eds), *Individual and Community Response to Trauma and Disaster: The Structure of Human Chaos* (Cambridge: Cambridge University Press, 1994), p. 312.

19 'Keep them close to the tribe', i.e. keep troubled soldiers near the units, was also a motto in the Iraq War. *The New York Times*, 4 April 2003.

20 For a detailed analysis of the breakdowns in the last-century wars see, Ben Shephard, *A War of Nerves: Soldiers and Psychiatrists in the Twentieth Century* (Cambridge, Mass.: Harvard University Press, 2000).

21 Lawrence Ingraham and Frederick Manning, 'American Military Psychiatry', in Richard A. Gabriel (ed.), *Military Psychiatry: A Comparative Perspective* (New York: Greenwood Press, 1986), p. 55.

22 More on traumas after Vietnam war in Jonathan Shay, *Achilles in Vietnam: Combat Trauma and the Undoing of the Character* (New York: Atheneum, 1994).

23 Wendy Holden, *Shell Shock: The Psychological Impact of War*. (London: Channel 4 Books, 1998), p. 171.

24 Ibid., p. 172.

25 This reflection is quoted by Jim Goodwin, 'The etiology of combat-related traumatic stress-disorder', www.trauma-papers.org.

26 Lacanian psychoanalysis does not translate the French term *jouissance* with 'enjoyment', since the latter does not depict enough pleasure coupled with pain.

27 The melancholic is often with his or her lamenting accusing the other for leaving him: 'If the melancholic says, "I'm a mess", it should be understood as, "You are a mess". Sometimes we even hear something

like, "Why did you die on me?"' Roberto Harari, *Lacan's Seminar on 'Anxiety': An Introduction* (New York: The Other Press, 2001).

28 For a detailed description of killing in the last-century wars, see Joanna Bourke, *The Intimate History of Killing* (London: Granta, 1999). In analysing killing manuals, Bourke quotes from Norman Demuth, *Harrying the Hun: A Handbook of Scouting, Stalking and Camouflage* (London, 1941), p. 84; and M. D. S. Armour, *Total War Training for Home Guard Officers and N.C.O.s* (London, 1942), p. 46; PRO WO199/799, 'Realism in Army Training. The Spirit of Hate', undated newspaper clipping, and *The Times*, 27 April 1942, p. 2.

29 Bourke, ibid. Bourke refers here to Colonel R. G. Pollard, '6th Aust. Div. Training Instruction No.1 Jungle Warfare', 27 March 1943, p. 1, in *Lieutenant General Sir F.H. Berryman's papers*, AWM PR84/370 item 41, 1943.

30 Bourke, ibid., p. 100. The quote refers to Major Jules V. Coleman's psychoanalytic study of group relations, 'The group factor in military Psychiatry', *American Journal of Orthopsychiatry*, 16 (1946), p. 222. Soldiers also selectively incorporated the psychological theories they became knowledgeable in, and especially liked to identify with the theories which present killing as a natural instinctual thing, which helped them perceive killing as an emotionally transient event. The soldiers thus liked to say that they were not really killers, since they were just temporarily taken over by a murderous zeal and later returned to their normal selves.

31 Frederick Sadlier Brereton, *With Rifle and Bayonet: A Story of the Boer War* (London, 1900), p. 271.

32 Freud was also thinking about such possibility, saying that: 'The ideal solution, which medical men no doubt still yearn for, would be to discover some bacillus which could be isolated and bred in a pure culture and which, when injected into anyone, would invariably produce the same illness; or to put it rather less extravagantly, to demonstrate the existence of certain chemical substances the administration of which would bring about or cure particular neuroses. But the probability of a solution of this kind seems slight' ('Inhibition, symptoms and anxiety', p. 311).

33 See Franklin D. Jones, 'Future Directions of Military Psychiatry', in Richard A. Gabriel (ed.), *Military Psychiatry: A Comparative Perspective* (New York: Greenwood Press, 1986).

34 See Richard A. Gabriel, *The Painful Field: The Psychiatric Dimension of Modern War* (New York: Greenwood Press, 1988).

35 After the war in Afghanistan, which was mostly conducted at night-time, American soldiers supposedly started using the drug Provigil, which is marketed as medicine for chronic sleepiness. Since future wars will also require soldiers to be awake for long periods of time, scientists are busy discovering new substances that can prevent sleep. Some are even hoping to detect a gene that control sleep and finds ways to modify it. Quoted from *Esquire* in *Delo*, 3 June 2003.

36 See the report on the possibility of creating a 'guilt-free soldier' in *The Village Voice*, 22–8 January 2003.

37 Ibid.

38 In the last decade, the power of the curator has increased enormously, so that a curator acts as an intermediary between the artists and the public, not only telling the audience what is art and what not, but also taking on the role of the one who in some way enjoys in the place of the audience. Austrian philosopher Robert Phaller has coined the term 'interpassivity' to describe the states in which the subject deposits enjoyment into an intermediary who enjoys in place of the subject. An example would be a man who constantly records films but never watches them, because the recorder was the intermediary which had already enjoyed the film for him. In contemporary art a curator is often such an intermediary into whom the audience deposits enjoyment of the art. When I enter an art show where I am not really sure what is supposed to be the artistic value of the works displayed, I presuppose that the curator saw something in the objects which makes them art in his eyes – I therefore take the curator as someone who enjoys art in my place. Going around the gallery, I can continue thinking about my lousy job or my personal dilemmas while the curator was the one who actually watched the art for me.

Curators today resemble the CNN journalists who are also present in a war like intermediaries who are exposing images of violence in front of our eyes and giving quick theories on the war. It is almost as if the reporters are watching the war instead of the public – the latter can then go on with their everyday lives while the TV deals with the suffering in their place. However, curators have also taken on a role of another type of intermediary – they more and more become successful businessmen who know how to market art and how to sell it. In the recent Internet debate on the question of what curators should do in time of war, a

German art critic has wisely suggested that businessmen usually feel unimportant in wartime, since decisions on war and peace are left to the generals and politicians. This critic was surprised that manager-curators wanted to go beyond art and to convert themselves into state-ments-curators, i.e. persons who are controlling the political frame-work of our civilization. The critic concluded with the question whether it is not time that we have normal, average, even banal curators; since artists have already discovered the strategies of banality, one won-ders when will curators discover them.

39 For a very lucid account on the representation of violence in today's media, see, Stanley Cohen, *States of Denial: Knowing About Atrocities and Suffering* (Cambridge: Polity Press, 2001).

40 For the analysis of the Gulf War Syndrome as a new form of hysteria, see Elaine Showalter, *Hystories* (New York: Columbia University Press, 1998).

41 The American military has in the past years supposedly used anti-anthrax vaccination for soldiers dispatched to the Middle East, since there existed fear that Iraq might use anthrax as a biological weapon. But according to a 15 January 1999 article in *The Baltimore Sun*, internal Department of Defence documents indicate that half the pilots in some Air Guard squadrons were resigning or seeking non-flying jobs to avoid having to take the vaccine. Analysts of the Gulf War Syndrome, like Michael Fumento, blame this behaviour on a mixture of old-fashioned mass paranoia, conspiracy theorists, media sensationalism, congres-sional demagogues, and a powerful new weapon of mass disinformation, the Internet. More on this on http://www.fumento.com.

THREE   SUCCESS IN FAILURE

1 *The Sunday Times, Style Magazine*, 15 Sept. 2002.

2 For an analysis of how the ideology of the 'new money and being yourself' was linked to the success and failure of the 1990s dot.com business, see Thomas Frank, *One Market Under God: Extreme Capitalism, Market Populism, and the End of Economics Democracy* (New York: Anchor Books, 2000).

3 See Soeren Kierkegaard, *The Concept of Anxiety*, trans. R. Thomte and A. B. Anderson (Princeton: Princeton University Press, 1980).

4 Ibid., pp. 42–3.

5 Jean Paul Sartre makes a similar point about anxiety by taking the example of a man standing on top of a cliff. What is horrifying for this man is not the possibility of falling, but the fact that he has the power to jump into the abyss. See his *Being and Nothingness: A Phenomenological Essay on Ontology*, trans. Hazel E. Bernes (New York: Taylor and Francis Books Ltd., 2002).

6 The inability to make decisions is referred to also as 'buridantis'. See http://www.oprah.com/health/omag/health_omag_200101_reinven.jhtml

7 See *The New York Times*, 27 Aug. 2000.

8 Ibid.

9 See Sigmund Freud, 'Group psychology and the analysis of the ego', *The Pelican Freud Library*, vol. 10 (London, Penguin, 1985). Paradoxically it was Freud's nephew, Edward Bernays, who became known as the father of public relations. His book, *Propaganda* in 1928 promoted advertising as the primary mode of communication. As a representative of Lucky Strike, Bernays became known as the person who helped to break the ban on women smoking in public. His marketing strategy was to organize a contingent of women to ostentatiously puff 'torches of freedom' during a parade.

10 See Naomi Klein, *No Logo* (London: Flamingo, 2001).

11 Jackson Lears, *Fables of Abundance: A Cultural History of Advertising in America* (New York: Basic Books, 1994), pp 139, 208.

12 Recently, there has been a boom of such coffee places in Japan. Consumers there explain that in the past they used to frequent bars and tea houses after work in order to avoid going home, but now they go to Starbucks because it feels more like home. Of course, this fake home is a calm oasis without screaming children and nagging spouse.

13 On how this experience economy affects tourism, see Dean MacCannell, *The Tourist* (Los Angeles: UCLA Press, 1999).

14 Jeremy Rifkin, *The Age of Access* (New York: J. P. Tarcher, 2001), p. 7.

15 Ibid., p. 29.

16 Ibid., p. 30.

17 See Darian Leader, *Why Do Women Write More Letters Than They Send? A Meditation on the Loneliness of the Sexes* (New York: Basic Books, 1997).

18 Ben Cheever, *Selling Ben Cheever* (New York: Bloomsbury Publishing, 2001), p. 99. On the same theme, see also Barbara Ehrenreich, *Nickel and*

Dimed: On (Not) Getting By in America (New York: Metropolitan Books, 2001).

19 Fran Abrams, *Below the Breadline: Living on the Minimum Wage* (London: Profile Books, 2002), p. 1.

20 Ibid., p. 7.

21 Ibid., p. 5. Ehrenreich has a much more politically conscious view and points out that the poor severely lack civil liberties and that they are living in a particular type of dictatorship: 'My guess is that the indignities imposed on so many low-wage workers – the drug tests, the constant surveillance, being "reamed out" by managers – are part of what keeps wages low. If you're made to feel unworthy enough, you may come to think that what you're paid is what you are actually worth' (*Nickel and Dimed*, p. 211)

22 Polly Toynbee in *Hard Work: Life in Low-pay Britain* (London: Bloomsbury, 2003) gives the most leftist account of how the poor live by pointing out the demise of the trade unions and the political confidence that the proletarians used to have in the past: 'Even if the poorer worker were always on the underside of that class and largely ignored by the strong trade unions, by hanging on to the idea of a united working class, gripping its coat-tails, they too could feel represented by its class Politics' (pp. 226–7).

23 Cheever, *Selling Ben Cheever*, pp. xviii–xix.

24 *The New York Times Magazine*, 13 April 2003.

25 The new reality shows that depict how ordinary family life today resembles sit-coms are openly admitting how today people's everyday lives are shaped in accordance to the movies and not vice versa.

26 See Frank Furedi, *Paranoid Parenting* (Chicago: Chicago Review Press, 2002).

FOUR   LOVE ANXIETIES

1 Women have in the past frequently sent Valentine cards to themselves in order to be able to display them in their apartment or office and thus incite jealousy of the others. Although here one can easily see that the subject makes such gestures to elicit a response from the Other, sending an e-greeting to one's own computer appears much more of a solitary act. However, a computer, too, can be taken as a big Other – a new type of symbolic space.

2 Edmond Rostand, *Cyrano de Bergerac*, trans. Gladys Thomas and Mary F. Guillemand (http://ibiblio.org/gutenberg/etext98/cdben10.txt).

3 Ibid.

4 Here one needs to look at Lacan's formulas of sexuation, especially their lover part. One finds on the male side a split subject and the phallus. There is no direct link between the phallus and the split subject: the subject has a relation only to object *a* on the female side of the formulas. And on the female side, one finds three elements: a barred Woman, who has a relation to the phallus on the side of man and to a barred Other, while she has no relation to object *a*, which is on her side of the formulas. See, Jacques Lacan, *On Feminine Sexuality: The Limits of Love and Knowledge (Seminar XX, 1972/3)*, transl. Bruce Fink, New York, Norton, 1998). See also, *Reading Seminar XX, Lacan's Major Work on Love, Knowledge and Feminine Sexuality*, ed. Susan Barnard and Bruce Fink (Albany, NY: SUNY Press, 2002).

5 Jacques Lacan, *Angoisse* (unpublished seminar), 5 June 1963.

6 Ibid., 26 March 1963.

7 Ibid.

8 Ibid.

9 Jacques-Alain Miller, *H2O: Suture in Obsessionality* (http:www.lacan.com/suturef.htm).

10 Paul Julian Smith, *Desire Unlimited: The Cinema of Pedro Almodovar* (London: Verso, 1994), p. 81.

11 Psychotics often function very well in society, because they have a great ability to mimic the behaviour of others around them. More on psychosis in Genevieve Morel, *Ambiguités sexuelles: Sexuation et psychose* (Paris: Economica, 2000).

12 Ibid.

13 See Jacques Lacan, *On Feminine Sexuality: The Limits of Love and Knowledge (Seminar XX, 1972/3)*, trans. Bruce Fink (New York: Norton, 1998).

14 See, *Libération*, 20 and 21 Aug. 1983

15 The seduction that such a Cyrano can engage in on the Internet can, of course, create quite a havoc in women's lives. At the time of the war in Afghanistan, Colonel Kassem Saleh engaged in numerous Internet affairs with women who were most charmed by his prose. He was a tall, good-looking, special forces officer contacting women from the war zone and was able to write messages that women 'found as intoxicating

as a crystal flute of champagne'. And he seemed to be so different from other commitment-phobic men, since he often quickly asked women to marry him, forgetting, of course, that he was already married. While this story sounds nothing new in today's times, what is more paradoxical is that when the story of this online Lothario was revealed on TV, some women who were in love with him, decided to search for their legal rights and demand some repayment for their suffering. As one woman says: 'We are not a group of stupid, naïve women. . . . We are bright, intellectual, professional women. I can't tell you how much he wooed us with his words. He made us feel like goddesses, fairy princesses, Cinderellas. We had all found our Superman, our knight in shining armor' (*Independent*, 12 June 2003). Is the fact that women still today so much need a Cyrano and that many men are willing to create a mirror in which women appear likeable to themselves grounds for legal action? And if so, what kind of a repayment would sufficiently compensate for the broken mirror?

FIVE   ANXIETY OF MOTHERHOOD

1 *Houston Chronicle*, 6 March 2002.

2 *Time Magazine*, 20 Jan. 2002.

3 See Otto Rank, *The Trauma of Birth* (London: K. Paul, Trench, Trubner, 1929). Rank considered all subject's later attacks of anxiety to be an attempt to deal with the trauma of birth.

4 See Freud, 'Inhibitions, Symptoms and Anxiety'. If Freud in his earlier texts like *The Interpretation of Dreams* (SE vols 4 and 5), *Introductory Lectures on Psycho-Analysis* (SE 15 and 16), and even in *The Ego and the Id* (SE 19), briefly mentions that birth is the first great anxiety state, in 'Inhibitions, Symptoms and Anxiety' he develops a radical critique of Rank.

5 The subject often tries to get this pound of flesh back by way of taking it from someone else. After certain crimes the perpetrator, for example, tears a piece of body from the victim and sometimes even preserves it. Taking the scalp of the victim or even the heart has been part of violent encounters in many cultures. Even in recent wars victors often take a memento from their enemy, either in the form of a piece of body or a symbolic token (jewellery, purse, diary). With such gestures it is as if the perpetrator tries to get back what has been lacking to him or herself.

6 When a man kills his children, this is usually explained in the context of

him being either psychotic or under the influence of alcohol or drugs, while when women commit such acts, it often seems that the law does not search for such explanations. Most horrifying when women commit such crimes seems to be the very lack of any attempt by them to justify their act. When they kill children, men often kill their wives too.

7 See Jacques-Alain Miller, 'On Semblances in the Relation Between the Sexes,' in Renata Salecl (ed.), *Sexuation* (Durham: Duke University Press, 2000), p. 18.

8 Miller nicely observes that the church had discovered true women before psychoanalysis: 'It saw in them a threat and developed a solution: marry them off to God.' These are the women who take the vows of obedience, poverty and chastity for life. Here the feminine lack-of-having comes to term with vows which seem to frame feminine *jouissance*: 'They reveal that no man can be at this level of jouissance, and that no one less than God himself is needed here' (Ibid., p. 23).

9 Susan Smith had a history of sexual abuse, as well as various sexual relationships with men who seem to represent authority in her life, which obviously opens up lots of questions about her sexuality, which seems to alternate between the role of the victim and seductress. When she started serving her prison sentence, she also had two sexual relationships with guards.

10 *Time Magazine*, 28 Jan. 2002.

11 In explaining her attempted suicide to the psychologist, Andrea claimed that suicide was for her a way of heading off what the visions and voices were leading to. She thus said: 'I had a fear I would hurt somebody. I thought it better to end my own life and prevent it' (Ibid.).

12 Ibid.

13 *Houston Chronicle*, 6 March 2002.

14 'Yates' Preacher Warned of Hellfire' was reported on the *ABCNews.com* (http://www.beliefnet.com/story/103/story_10342.html).

15 More on this in Renata Salecl, *The Spoils of Freedom: Psychoanalysis and Feminism After the Fall of Socialism* (London: Routledge, 1994).

16 *The New York Times*, 24 Feb. 2002.

17 At the trial, the influence of religion becomes quite obvious. The psychiatrist Dr Park Diaz, who was hired by the prosecutors to show how Yates knew right from wrong made a judgement that Yates did not do things that 'he would have expected a loving mother to do if she

believed she was saving them from hell. "She doesn't tell them they'll be with Jesus or God," he said. "She doesn't offer words of comfort" ' (*Houston Chronicle*, 8 March 2002).

The defence in its appeal also pointed out that Dr Diaz testified that Yates may have got the idea for her crime from a television show *Law and Order* about a woman who drowned her children and was acquitted by reason of insanity. However, a few days after Yates was convicted it was discovered that this show never happened (*Houston Chronicle*, 4 April 2002).

18 See Grant H. Morris and Ansar Haroun, MD, ' "God Told Me to Kill": Religion or Delusion', *San Diego Law Review*, 38: 973 (1999), p. 1008

19 Jacques Lacan, *The Four Fundamental Concepts of Psycho-Analysis* (New York: W. W. Norton and Co., 1981), p. 263

20 See Sigmund Freud's case history of Schreber in 'Psychoanalytic notes upon an autobiographical account of a case of paranoia (dementia paranoids)', (*SE* 12)

21 A psychotic's relationship with her own body differs from that of the neurotic's. The latter's body has been changed by language in such a way that *jouissance* has been extracted from it and only appears in the pockets of the partial drives, while a psychotic's body is invaded by *jouissance*. Andrea Yates's possession by the devil can also be perceived as such an invasion by *jouissance*. For more on the difference between neurosis and psychosis see Bruce Fink, *A Clinical Introduction to Lacanian Psychoanalysis: Theory and Technique* (Cambridge Mass.: Harvard University Press, 1997). Fink also notes that for a neurotic it is often most difficult to act directly and effectively, while a psychotic can quickly react to the slightest provocation.

22 Herbert A. Schreier and Judith A. Libow, *Hurting for Love: Munchausen by Proxy Syndrome* (New York and London: The Guilford Press, 1993), p. 45.

23 'His diet reportedly consisted entirely of breast milk expressed from the mother and a neighbor, sourdough bread, and a liquid diet supplement. He was on a regimen of 11 different medications and exhibited complications associated with prolonged administration of huge toxic doses of corticosteroids, ostensibly prescribed by someone for asthma' (Ibid).

24 Ibid., p. 48.

25 Catherine Mathelin, *Lacanian Psychotherapy with Children* (New York: The Other Press, 1999), p. 30.

26 Ibid., p. 31.

27 Ibid., p. 32.

28 In psychoanalysis of children it has been noted that when the child is very aggressive and unruly, it is often that the child tries with his behaviour to distract his mother from depression. It is as if the child tries to keep his mother occupied so that she has no time to fall into depression.

29 In popular psychology we, on the one hand, have the perception that people can be advised how to express themselves fully, how they can learn to be able to utter their inner feelings, desires etc., but, on the other hand, we have advice that teaches people how to 'deceive' each other so that they will be able to get what they want (here I have in mind various self-help books on how to succeed in love, work, etc.).

30 One is quite surprised how little media attention has been given to the case of a Californian man, Adair Garcia, who at the time of the Yates trial, killed five of his six children with a barbecue grill and tried to commit suicide himself. The media guessed that the man had been depressed because his wife seemed to have left him; however they did not probe more into the fact that he showed no emotions after he was resuscitated in the hospital and had a 'blank, pale look on his face'. Depression seems to be today the term one can stretch in all possible directions in order to understand the cause of crime.

31 See Darian Leader, 'Sur l'ambivalence maternelle', in *Savoirs et clinique*, 1 (March 2002).

SIX CAN TESTIMONY OFFER A CURE FOR ANXIETY?

1 *The New York Times*, 23 Feb. 2003.

2 Ibid.

3 Freud, 'Inhibitions, symptoms, and anxiety', p. 326

4 Ibid.

5 Ibid., p. 327

6 Jankl appears as the first good father-figure.

7 Binjamin Wilkomirski, *Fragments* (New York: Schocken Books, 1996), p. 78.

8 Ibid., p. 3.

9 Ibid., p. 125.

10 Ibid., pp. 6–7.

11 See Elena Lappin, 'The man with two heads', *Granta*, 66 (1999). See also Philip Gourevitch, 'The memory thief', *The New Yorker*, 14 June 1999.

12 http://www.english.upenn.edu/~afilreis/Holocaust/children-camps-bk-review.html

13 If we compare this distinction between reality and fiction with September 11, we find a particular reversal. For Wilkomirski, the traumatic event is something real, but the outside world is not while, at the time of September 11, it looked as if the very event was just a fiction.

14 *Fragments*, p. 154

15 Ibid., p. 155

16 For a detailed analysis of his change in the belief in the big Other, see Renata Salecl, *(Per)versions of Love and Hate* (London: Verso, 1998).

17 Freud, 'Inhibitions, symptoms and anxiety', p. 326. Martin Heidegger also took preparedness for anxiety as something that allows the subject to differently relate to his own finitude. See his *Being and Time*, trans. J. Macquarrie and E. Robinson (Oxford: Basil Blackwell, 1962).

18 Cf. Jacques Lacan, *The Seminar of Jacques Lacan, Book 1* (New York: Norton, 1993), p. 191.

19 Cf. Lawrence L. Langer, *Holocaust Testimonies: The Ruins of Memory* (New Haven: Yale University Press, 1991), p. 5.

20 Shoshanna Felman and Dori Laub, M.D., *Testimony: Crises of Witnessing in Literature, Psychoanalysis, and History* (New York: Routledge), 1992, p. 81.

21 Ibid., pp. 81, 82.

22 For the analysis of this trend, see Robert Hughes, *Culture of Complaint: A Passionate Look into the Ailing Heart of America* (New York: Warner Books, 1994).

23 Stefan Maechler in his book, *The Wilkomirski Affair: A Study in Biographical Truth*, trans. John F. Woods (New York: Schocken Books, 2001) points out an interesting reaction to Wilkomirski's book that goes very much hand in hand with our culture of complaint: a Swiss lawyer presumably sued Wilkomirski when he learned that the book was a fraud. The lawyer did not simply want to recover money for the book, but a compensation for being maliciously tricked into feeling sympathy for its subject matter.

24 Here one can compare Schreber's traumas with his very authoritarian father, which also contributed to the son's fall into psychosis.

25 J. Hoberman in his critique of the film claims that one would not be

able to make such a 'simple fable' of paternal self-sacrifice set in a Serbian concentration camp or in the killing fields of Rwanda. However, we need to remember that most films that dealt with the Bosnian war involved precisely the idea of a good father figure. In *Welcome to Sarajevo* this is the British journalist who rescues a Bosnian girl; in *Patriot* George Clooney . . . . The impotence of the authorities only comes to surface in *No Man's Land*, where there seems to be no one who can rescue the men caught in the hell of the nationalist struggle on top of the ticking bomb. See J. Hoberman, 'Dreaming the unthinkable', *Sight and Sound* 2 (Feb. 1999), p. 23. For another view on *Life is Beautiful*, see also Slavoj Zizek, *The Fragile Absolute* (London: Verso, 2000).

26 Darian Leader, *Promises Lovers Make When It Gets Late* (London: Faber and Faber, 1998).

27 See Maechler, *The Wilkomirski Affair*.

SEVEN CONCLUSION

1   The attack on September 11 has introduced an unease about the imaginary depiction of reality. The image of the falling twin towers, for example, had to be repeated on TV again and again in order to be taken as something real, since for the audience it was hard to realize that it was not just another movie. *Entertainment Weekly* nicely described how people viewed the collapse of the WTC: 'We saw it, and then we saw it again. We saw it over and over, but there was still no way to accept it as real. We went numb for a while, we drifted into a zone where we could barely absorb all of the data flushing and scrolling over the TV screen, but then we saw the image for the 14th time, or the 37th, or the 112th, and that's when it punctured our hearts. That is when we knew it was real, and that's when we started to wonder whether we would ever stop seeing it' (*Entertainment Weekly*, 28 Sept. 2001).

2   http://womencetral.msn.com/relationships/articles/LTV2.asp

3   See Paul-Laurent Assoun, *L'Angoisse* (Paris, Economica, 2002), p. 95.

4   The theme of reinvention is present in many domains of our lives. The *New York Times* reported on a growing number of American executives who lost their jobs in recent years and who have followed different ways of reinventing themselves. One job-seeker who has been through numerous networking meetings, job counselling, self-help groups and image advising, while feeling completely tired of this machinery, still

says: 'I am looking for a conclusion here . . . I would like to get this thing resolved so I can rebuild my identity and get on with my life' (*The New York Times Magazine*, 13 April 2003).

5   More on this in Renata Salecl, *The Spoils of Freedom*.

6   See Theodor W. Adorno and Max Horkheimer, *Dialectic of Enlightenment*, trans. Edmund Jephcott (Stanford: Stanford University Press, 2002).

Some of the ideas in Chapter 3 were first published in *Parallax*, Vol. 9 (April–June 2002, No. 2); an early version of Chapter 4 appeared in Todd McGowan and Sheila Kunke (eds.), *Lacan and Contemporary Film* (New York: The Other Press, 2004); and a version of Chapter 5 was published in *Cardozo Law Review*, Vol. 24 (August 2003, No. 6).

Index

cultural capitalism and 63–7; economic development 11–13

Propaganda (Bernays) 157n

psychoanalytic theory: on anxiety 17–18; deprivation of *jouissance* 30; desire of Other 24–8; Freud 18–21; Lacan's Other 21–3; obessional desire and 81–4; soldiers and killing 35–6, 39; trauma and parenthood 97–9; Yates and 105

psychosis and neurosis: body relationship 162n; legal guilt and 96–7

psychotherapy: recovered memories 137–8; for war experiences 39

Quinn, Mark 41

Ramsey, Gordon 146

Rank, Otto 98

relationships 14 *see also* love; parenthood

religion: loss of faith in 2; quest for certainty 5 *see also* Yates, Andrea

Rifkin, Jeremy: *The Age of Access* 59–60

Riviere, Joan 21

robots and simulacra: in art 43, 44; immortality with 48

role confusion 4–5

Rostand, Edmond: *Cyrano de Bergerac* 75, 78–81, 84–6

Saleh, Colonel Kassem 159–60n

Sartre, Jean Paul 156–7n

Schreber, Judge 110, 162n 165n

secrets: parents and children 114–18

Seminar I (Lacan) 131

September 11 *see* terrorism

sexuality: Freudian theory and 18–21; homosexuality 86–8; Lacan on 159n

Shannabrook, Richard 44

Slovenia 11

Smith, Paul Julian 87–8

Smith, Susan 100–2, 161n

So, Vu Quang 33–4

social class 63–7

Solomon, Zahava 152n

Stelarc 42, 43, 45

suicide: melancholy soldiers 29, 31–3

survival: guilt over 31–2

Survivor (television) 67

Tabor, Ive 44

television: 'reality' shows 67–9

terrorism 2–3; cells structure 9; children and 150n; de-briefing 119; falling twin towers 165n; government speculation about 7–9; media portrayal 143; solidarity with victims 12; surviving 119–20; vulnerability to 5–6

They Came From Within (film) 7

Toynbee, Polly: *Hard Work* 158n

trauma: birth 96–9; compassionate fixer 130; de-briefing strategies 119–21; and events 130–1; fictionalizing 138–40; link to